The Young Coder's Python Adventure

Tamim Shahriar

Copyright © 2024 Tamim Shahriar

All rights reserved. No part of this book may be reproduced or used in any manner without the prior written permission of the copyright owner, except as permitted by copyright law.

ISBN: 9798332994609
First Published: July 2024

Cover art by Naeem Ahmed
Edited by Mosharraf Hosain

To Aarav and Onora

Contents

Chapter	Page
Welcome to Your Python Adventure!	7
Chapter 1 – Discovering the Turtle Module	11
Chapter 2 – Drawing with the Turtle	23
Chapter 3 – Bulls-Eye Coding: Creating a Target Board	32
Chapter 4 – Illuminating Traffic Lights with Python	37
Chapter 5 – Crafting a Colorful Rainbow	44
Chapter 6 – Keyboard Adventures with the Turtle	50
Chapter 7 – Let's Play a Guessing Game	54
Chapter 8 – Clicking Creativity: Drawing Shapes with the Mouse	58
Chapter 9 – Turtle Derby: Racing to the Finish Line	66
Chapter 10 – Timekeeper: Building a Digital Wall Clock	70
Chapter 11 – RGB in Action: Creating New Colors Through Code	78
Chapter 12 – Crack the Code: Unveiling the Caesar Cipher	90
Chapter 13 – Unmasking the Mystery: Play Hangman	96
Chapter 14 – Beyond Guessing Games: Exploring Binary Search	105
Chapter 15 – Memory Number Game: Test Your Working Memory!	109

Chapter 16 – Ready, Set, Throw! Play Rock, Paper, Scissors with Your Computer	113
Chapter 17 – Interactive Movement: Steering a Robot on the Grid	117
Chapter 18 – X's and O's Take the Stage: Building Tic Tac Toe with Python	128

Welcome to Your Python Adventure!

Learning the basics of programming can be surprisingly fast! In just 6-8 weeks (or 80-100 hours), you'll be ready to build cool projects. The key? Making it fun!

This book focuses on creating projects that are both entertaining and challenging. You won't just be copying and pasting code – you'll be using your new skills to solve problems and unleash your creativity.

Why did I write this book? Because when I taught programming at *Tamim's ThinkLab*, I realized there weren't many resources that offered this kind of fun, hands-on learning. So, I created this book for you, whether you're my student or anyone else who wants to learn Python in a way that sticks.

Get ready to have a blast while you code! Just like me, I hope you find learning with joy is the best way to learn for good.

Who Is This Book For?

Before you start, make sure you have Python installed on your computer. You should be able to write and run simple Python programs on your own. This book is not for beginners who have never programmed before. Before reading this book, you should have a basic understanding of Python programming concepts, including data types and variables, mathematical operations, conditional logic, loops, lists, dictionaries, sets, and tuples. You should also be able to write a small program and run it on your computer.

This book is for those who want to take their Python programming skills to the next level by creating fun and engaging projects. It assumes you have some basic programming experience and are ready to dive into more challenging tasks.

How to Use This Book?

To get the most out of this book, it's important to follow the chapters in the order they are presented. Each chapter builds on the concepts from the previous ones, ensuring that you develop a solid understanding as you progress.

Take your time and think critically as you read. It's tempting to rush through the material, but programming is best learned through careful and thoughtful practice. Make sure to read the code examples carefully. Instead of just glancing over them, type out the code and run it on your computer. This hands-on approach will help you understand how the code works.

Don't worry if you don't understand everything at first. The key is to get the programs to run correctly. As you become more comfortable, try modifying the code and experimenting to see what happens. This process of trial and error is not only more fun but also a highly effective way to learn. Experimenting on your own can often be more educational than immediately asking for help or searching online for answers.

As you work through each new program, try to connect it to the concepts from previous chapters. This will help reinforce your understanding and build a cohesive knowledge base. By experimenting and exploring on your own, you'll gain a deeper and more lasting understanding of Python programming.

Remember, the most important thing is to engage actively with the material. Read thoughtfully, type out and run the code, and don't be afraid to experiment and ask questions. By doing so, you'll not only learn Python but also enjoy the process of discovering and creating with code.

This page intentionally left blank

Chapter 1

Discovering the Turtle Module

Welcome to an exciting part of your Python adventure! In this chapter, we're going to introduce you to a fantastic Python module called *turtle*. It's built right into Python, so you can use it without any extra downloads. No time to waste – let's fire up Python's IDLE and write our very first program together!

Here's a simple program to get us started:

```python
import turtle

t = turtle.Turtle()

t.forward(100)
t.right(60)
t.backward(100)

turtle.done()
```

Once you've crafted your turtle program, it's time to save and run it. Remember, don't name your file "turtle.py" – this will cause an error. Save your file with a unique name using the ".py" extension.

If everything's in order, hit the run button and watch the turtle magic unfold! You should see something drawn on your screen, just like the one in the picture below:

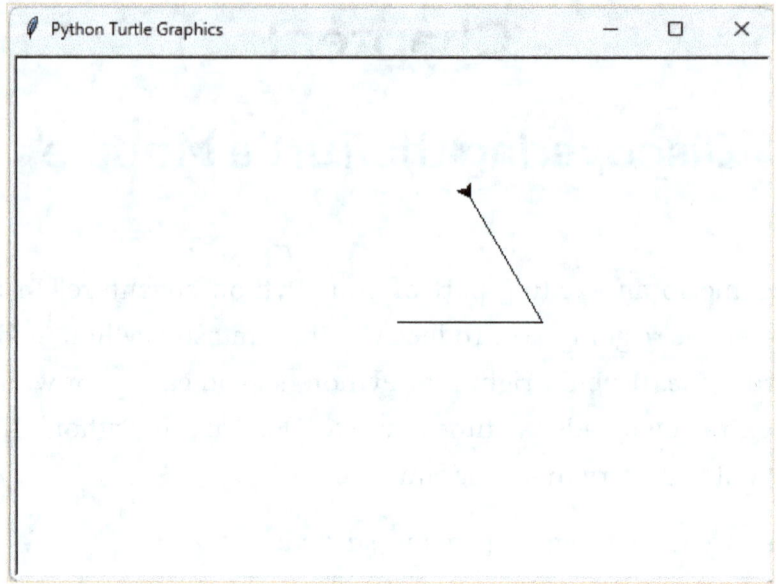

Let's break down the code and understand what each line does:

Importing the Turtle Module

`import turtle`

This line imports the turtle module into our program. Think of modules as specialized toolboxes that provide us with useful functions. By importing the turtle module, we gain access to its drawing capabilities.

Creating a Turtle Object

`t = turtle.Turtle()`

This line creates a turtle object, which is essentially a digital pen that we'll use to draw on the screen. We assign this object to a variable named t for easy reference.

Sending commands to the turtle

`t.forward(100)`

Now comes the fun part! We're telling our turtle t to move forward 100 steps using the `forward()` method. This method takes a distance as an argument and instructs the turtle to move that distance in a straight line. The `forward()` method is like a magic spell for our turtle. We don't need to worry about the internal workings of how it makes the turtle move; the turtle module handles that for us. We simply provide the distance, and the turtle takes care of the rest.

Next Step: Turning and Moving Back

```
t.right(60)
t.backward(100)
```

The `right(60)` method tells the turtle to turn right by 60 degrees. After turning, the `backward(100)` method makes the turtle move backward by 100 steps.

Keeping the Window Open

Finally, the line `turtle.done()` keeps the turtle graphics window open until you close it. This allows you to see the drawing your turtle has created. There are other ways to achieve this, which we shall see later in the book.

You might be wondering why we see an arrow-shaped icon instead of an actual turtle. The turtle module uses an arrow by default to represent the turtle's direction. However, we can customize the turtle's appearance to resemble a real turtle if we wish. Let's enhance our turtle program with some new tricks:

```python
import turtle

t = turtle.Turtle()

t.shape("turtle")
t.pencolor("red")

t.forward(100)
t.right(60)
t.backward(100)

turtle.done()
```

In this enhanced version of our turtle program, we're introducing two new tricks:

1. Shaping Up: A Turtle for Real

Using the `shape()` method, we're giving our turtle a makeover. Now, instead of the default arrow icon, we'll see a real turtle on the screen!

The turtle module offers several shapes that you can use to customize the appearance of your turtle. Here are some of the shapes you can try:

- *Arrow:* This is the default shape.
- *Turtle:* A classic turtle shape.
- *Circle:* A simple circular shape.
- *Square:* A square shape.
- *Triangle:* A triangular shape.

- *Classic:* The original turtle shape from early turtle graphics.

You can change the shape of your turtle by using the `shape()` method with one of these shape names as the argument. For example:

```
# change to "arrow", "turtle", "square",
# "triangle", or "classic"
t.shape("circle")
```

2. A Splash of Color: Red Lines

With the `pencolor()` method, we're adding a touch of personality to our turtle's strokes. The lines it draws will now be a vibrant red, making the drawing more eye-catching.

The rest of the program remains the same, with our turtle moving forward, turning right, and moving backward, creating a simple drawing on the screen.

Now, it's your turn to get hands-on! Open your Python IDLE, type in the complete program, and hit the run button. Watch as your turtle takes shape and colors the screen with its red lines. Have fun experimenting with different shapes and colors!

Drawing a Triangle with Our Turtle

Let's use our turtle friend to create a classic shape: a triangle. Here's how we'll do it:

1. *Step Forward 100:* We'll start by instructing our turtle to move 100 steps forward using `t.forward(100)`. This will create the first side of our triangle.

2. *Turn Right 120 Degrees:* Now, it's time to change direction. We'll ask our turtle to turn 120 degrees to the right using `t.right(120)`. This sets the stage for the second side of the triangle.
3. *Repeat Steps 1 and 2:* We'll repeat the same steps we did before: `t.forward(100)` and `t.right(120)`. This will create the second and third sides of the triangle, completing its shape.

Here's the complete program to draw a triangle:

```python
import turtle

t = turtle.Turtle()

t.forward(100)
t.right(120)

t.forward(100)
t.right(120)

t.forward(100)

turtle.done()
```

Run the program, and voila! You'll see a beautiful triangle grace your screen. For those with a knack for math, here's a question to ponder: Why did we turn right 120 degrees twice in the program?

From Triangle to Quadrilateral: The Challenge Awaits

With triangles conquered, let's move on to quadrilaterals. Can you, the budding programmer, create a quadrilateral on your own? A special type of quadrilateral is a square, where all four sides are equal and each angle measures 90 degrees. Take up the challenge and create your very own square using turtle graphics.

Here's a hint to get you started:

1. *Step Forward:* Use the `t.forward(100)` method to draw the first side of the square.
2. *Turn Right:* Use the `t.right(90)` method to turn the turtle 90 degrees to the right.
3. *Repeat:* Repeat the above steps to draw all four sides of the square.

Remember, the beauty of programming lies in experimentation and exploration. So, go ahead, tweak the code, play with the angles and side lengths, and let your creativity shine through!

Loops: The Power of Repetition

Computers excel at performing tasks with speed and efficiency. In programming, we often encounter situations where we need to repeat a specific action multiple times. Instead of writing the same command repeatedly, we can harness the power of loops.

Introducing the 'for' Loop

The for loop is a versatile tool that allows us to execute a block of code repeatedly. It's like having a helper robot that tirelessly performs the same task for us.

The Syntax: A Simple Pattern

The syntax of the `for` loop is straightforward:

```
for _ in range(number_of_repetitions):
    # code to be repeated
```

In this structure:

- `_`: This is a placeholder variable that doesn't hold any value. It's simply used to keep track of the loop's progress.
- `range(number_of_repetitions)`: This part specifies how many times the loop should execute. For instance, if we replace `number_of_repetitions` with 10, the loop will run 10 times.
- `# code to be repeated`: This is where you write the code that you want to repeat. The loop will execute this code block for each iteration.

Drawing a Square with a Loop

Remember the square we drew earlier? Let's recreate it using a for loop:

```python
import turtle

t = turtle.Turtle()

for _ in range(4):
    t.forward(100)
    t.right(90)

turtle.done()
```

In this program, the loop runs four times (`range(4)`), and each time it moves the turtle forward 100 steps and turns it right 90 degrees. This creates a square on the screen.

Drawing a Pattern with a Loop

Now, let's create a pattern using a loop:

```python
import turtle

t = turtle.Turtle()

t.pencolor("green")

for _ in range(5):
    t.forward(150)
    t.right(144)

turtle.done()
```

> **Challenge**
>
> Before running the code, try to visualize the output on paper. What do you think the pattern will look like? Once you have an idea, run the code and see if your prediction is correct.

Indentation: A Crucial Aspect

In Python, indentation plays a vital role in defining code blocks. Notice how the code inside the for loop is slightly indented to the right. This indentation tells Python that these lines belong to the loop. Proper indentation is crucial for the correct execution of your code.

Embrace Loops, Explore Patterns

As you venture further into the world of programming, you'll discover a vast array of loops and their applications. Experiment with different loops, create captivating patterns, and unleash your programming creativity!

Lists: Bundling Up Multiple Items

In programming, we often deal with data. To reuse the same data repeatedly, we can store it in variables and then access it using those variables. For instance, we can write:

```python
steps = 100
t.forward(steps)
t.right(90)
t.forward(steps)
```

Similarly, we create a turtle object and store it in a variable named t before working with it:

```python
t = turtle.Turtle()
```

While variables can hold only one data item at a time, lists allow us to store multiple data items together. For example, to store a single color, we can write:

```python
color = "blue"
```

To store multiple colors, we can use a list:

```python
colors = ["red", "green", "blue", "orange"]
```

Here, `color` is a variable, while `colors` is a list. To access specific colors from the list, we use indexes. For instance, `colors[0]` will return "red", `colors[1]` will return "green", `colors[2]` will return "blue", and `colors[3]` will return "orange".

The numbers inside the square brackets are called indexes. Remember that indexes start from 0. So, to access the first item in the list, we use an index of 0.

Combining Lists and Loops: Colorful Squares

Now, let's combine lists and loops to create a colorful square:

```python
t = turtle.Turtle()

colors = ["red", "green", "blue", "orange"]
for color in colors:
    t.pencolor(color)
    for _ in range(4):
        t.forward(100)
        t.right(90)

turtle.done()
```

In this program, we use a loop within a loop. The outer loop iterates through the `colors` list, extracting one color at a time. For each color, the inner loop draws a square using that color.

In the previous program, we drew the same square repeatedly using different colors. But what if we want to see each square distinctly on the screen? We can achieve this by slightly rotating the turtle after drawing each square. Look at the image below:

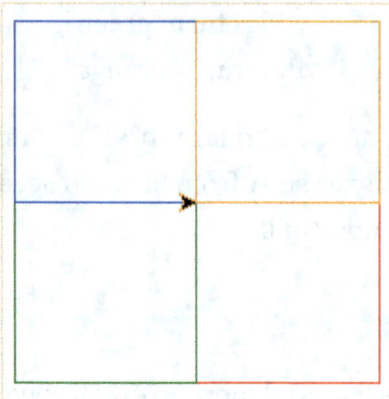

> **Challenge**
>
> Can you modify the program to create this effect?

Chapter 2

Drawing with the Turtle

In our previous chapter, we delved into the world of turtle graphics, exploring loops and lists along the way. Now, we're ready to embark on a new chapter of turtle-driven artistry, further expanding our programming horizons.

User Input: Empowering the Artist

Recall that we previously set the side length of our squares to 100 units. This time let's take it a step further and invite the user to input this value. Additionally, we'll allow the user to choose the color of their creation.

By incorporating user input, we're introducing a dynamic element into our programming. The user becomes an active participant, shaping the outcome of the program with their choices. This flexibility opens up a world of possibilities, allowing for personalized creations and interactive experiences.

As we embark on this journey of user-driven turtle graphics, remember that the key lies in understanding the user's perspective and providing a seamless interactive experience. Let's embrace the challenge and unleash our creativity!

Here's how you can do it:

```python
import turtle
```

```python
input_msg = "Enter the desired side length: "
side_length_str = input(input_msg)
side_length = int(side_length_str)

color = input("Enter the desired color: ")

t = turtle.Turtle()
t.pencolor(color)

for _ in range(4):
    t.forward(side_length)
    t.right(90)

turtle.done()
```

Now type and run the program. Notice the following key things:

- `side_length_str = input("Enter the desired side length: ")`: This line prompts the user to enter the desired side length of the square. The user's input is stored in the variable `side_length_str` as a string.
- `side_length = int(side_length_str)`: Since the program expects the side length to be a numerical value, we convert the string input (`side_length_str`) to an integer (`side_length`) using the `int()` function.
- `color = input("Enter the desired color: ")`: This line prompts the user to enter the desired color for the square. The user's input is stored in the variable `color` as a string.

Run the program and watch as your turtle creates a square based on the user's input. Experiment with different side lengths and colors to see how the turtle's drawing changes. Have fun exploring the power of user input in your turtle graphics!

Functions: What and Why?

In Python, we have a wealth of built-in functions readily available for our convenience. We'll gradually learn how to utilize these functions. However, we can also create our own functions. For instance, we can create a separate function to handle the task of drawing a square.

```python
import turtle


def draw_square(t, n):
    for _ in range(4):
        t.forward(n)
        t.right(90)


input_msg = "Enter the desired side length: "
side_length = input(input_msg)
side_length = int(side_length)

color = input("Enter the desired color: ")

t = turtle.Turtle()
t.pencolor(color)

draw_square(t, side_length)

turtle.done()
```

Now, whenever we need to draw a square within our program, we can simply call the `draw_square()` function. In programming terminology, calling a function is referred to as a function call.

Function Structure

When creating a function, we start with the `def` keyword, followed by the function name. Inside the parentheses after the function name, we can have one or more variables, known as parameters. These parameters are not mandatory; a function can be created without any parameters. Defining functions enhances code readability and organization.

Drawing Beyond Squares: Turtles and Creativity

Turtles aren't limited to drawing lines; they can create a variety of shapes. Let's write a program to draw a green circle with a blue interior. This time, the green outline will be slightly thicker than before. Observe the following program:

```python
import turtle

t = turtle.Turtle()

t.pensize(3)           # set the thickness of the outline
t.pencolor("green")    # set the color of the outline
t.fillcolor("blue")    # set the interior color

# move the turtle to the starting position
t.penup()
t.goto(0, -50)
t.pendown()
```

```
t.begin_fill()    # start filling the shape
t.circle(50)      # draw a circle with radius 50
t.end_fill()      # end filling the shape

turtle.done()
```

Now it's time to run the program on your computer. Watch as your turtle draws a green-outlined, blue-filled circle. Try experimenting with different colors and sizes to see what you can create. Enjoy the endless possibilities with your turtle!

2D Grid: Understanding Turtle Coordinates

The turtle draws on a two-dimensional grid. Each point on the screen can be represented by coordinates (x, y). The turtle starts at position (0, 0), meaning x = 0 and y = 0. As it moves to the right, the x value increases; to the left, it decreases. Similarly, moving upward increases the y value, while moving downward decreases it.

Turtle Position and Methods

To determine a turtle object's position, we use the `pos()` method. It returns the current x and y coordinates of the turtle object. To move the turtle to a specific location, we use the `goto()` method.

Exploring with a Program

Let's write a program to gain a deeper understanding of these concepts. First, carefully read the program and try to predict the output. Then, run the program and observe the results.

```
import turtle
```

```python
grid_turtle = turtle.Turtle()
grid_turtle.speed(1)
grid_turtle.penup()

x, y = grid_turtle.pos()
grid_turtle.write("x = {}, y = {}".format(x, y),
                  align="center",
                  font=("Arial", 14, "bold"))

grid_turtle.goto(200, 200)   # x = 200, y = 200
grid_turtle.pencolor("green")
grid_turtle.dot(15)
x, y = grid_turtle.pos()
grid_turtle.write("x = {}, y = {}".format(x, y),
                  align="center",
                  font=("Arial", 14, "bold"))

grid_turtle.goto(-200, -180)   # x = -200, y = -180
grid_turtle.pencolor("blue")
grid_turtle.dot(15)
x, y = grid_turtle.pos()
grid_turtle.write("x = {}, y = {}".format(x, y),
                  align="center",
                  font=("Arial", 14, "bold"))

grid_turtle.goto(-250, 250)   # x = -250, y = 250
grid_turtle.pencolor("red")
grid_turtle.dot(15)
x, y = grid_turtle.pos()
grid_turtle.write("x = {}, y = {}".format(x, y),
                  align="center",
                  font=("Arial", 14, "bold"))
```

```
grid_turtle.goto(250, -250)    # x = 250, y = -250
grid_turtle.pencolor("orange")
grid_turtle.dot(15)
x, y = grid_turtle.pos()
grid_turtle.write("x = {}, y = {}".format(x, y),
                  align="center",
                  font=("Arial", 14, "bold"))

turtle.done()
```

The simplest way to grasp the `penup()` method's function is to comment out the `grid_turtle.penup()` line using `# grid_turtle.penup()`. Then, rerun the program and observe the difference.

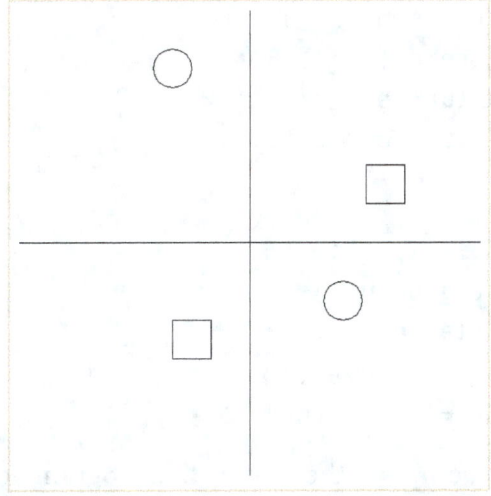

Your task is to write a program to draw the above image.

Here are some functions that you can use:

```
def draw_grid():
    # draw the x-axis
```

```python
    grid_turtle.penup()
    grid_turtle.goto(-300, 0)
    grid_turtle.pendown()
    grid_turtle.goto(300, 0)

    # draw the y-axis
    grid_turtle.penup()
    grid_turtle.goto(0, -300)
    grid_turtle.pendown()
    grid_turtle.goto(0, 300)

def draw_square(x, y):
    grid_turtle.penup()
    grid_turtle.goto(x, y)
    grid_turtle.pendown()
    for _ in range(4):
        grid_turtle.forward(50)
        grid_turtle.right(90)

def draw_circle(x, y):
    grid_turtle.penup()
    grid_turtle.goto(x, y)
    grid_turtle.pendown()
    grid_turtle.circle(25)
```

Will you try to complete the rest of the program yourself? If you can't do it even after trying for 20-25 minutes, you can look at the code below.

```python
# call the function to draw the grid
draw_grid()
```

```
# draw a square at (150, 100)
draw_square(150, 100)

# draw a circle at (120, -100)
draw_circle(120, -100)

# draw a square at (-100, -100)
draw_square(-100, -100)

# draw a circle at (-100, 200)
draw_circle(-100, 200)

grid_turtle.hideturtle()

turtle.done()
```

Awesome work! You've conquered user input, functions, and even the 2D grid. Keep on coding, and you'll be creating amazing things in no time!

Chapter 3

Bulls-Eye Coding: Creating a Target Board

Whether you're practicing with a bow and arrow or a firearm, a circular target board is essential. Hitting the bullseye, the centermost ring, earns the highest score. Points decrease as you move further away from the center. Even in the comfort of your home, you can find dartboard games to play. Today, we'll create a board for such a game, similar to the one shown in the image below:

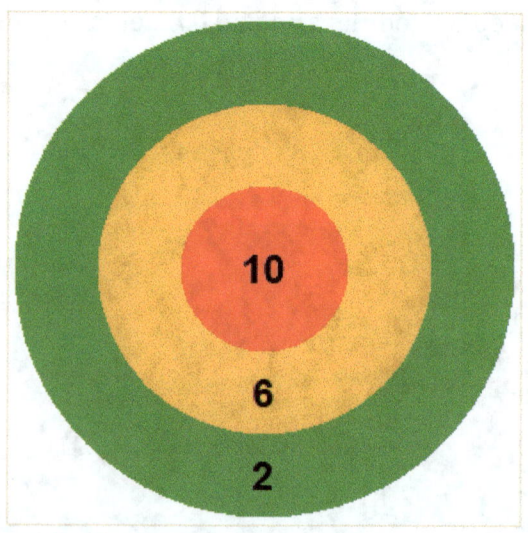

Scoring the Target: A Circle of Colors

In our target board, different colors represent different score zones:

- Red Zone: Hitting the red zone earns 10 points.
- Orange Zone: Landing in the orange zone is worth 6 points.
- Green Zone: A shot within the green zone scores 2 points.

Drawing the Target Rings

To create the target board, we'll draw three concentric circles, each with a different radius and color:

- *Red Circle:* The smallest circle with the smallest radius represents the highest-scoring zone (10 points).
- *Orange Circle:* A slightly larger circle with a slightly larger radius encloses the red circle, representing the 6-point zone.
- *Green Circle:* The largest circle with the largest radius encompasses the red and orange circles, representing the 2-point zone.

Imagine drawing the red circle first, then overlaying the orange circle with a slightly larger radius, and finally adding the green circle with the largest radius. What do you see?

Try the following Python program to see how it works:

```python
import turtle

t = turtle.Turtle()

t.dot(100, "red")
```

```
t.dot(200, "orange")
t.dot(300, "green")

turtle.done()
```

Do you see any problem with the code above? How can we solve it? Now close the book, look at the program on your computer and try to come up with a solution.

Here is the solution: If we draw the largest circle first, then the medium circle on top of it, and then the smallest circle on top of those, we will see all three circles – exactly like a dartboard. We can hide the turtle using `t.hideturtle()` to remove its mark.

```
import turtle

t = turtle.Turtle()

t.dot(300, "green")
t.dot(200, "orange")
t.dot(100, "red")

t.hideturtle()

turtle.done()
```

Running the program will now produce the output shown in the image below.

Chapter 3 – Bulls-Eye Coding: Creating a Target Board

Adding Scores to the Target

The next step is to display the scores. We need to write them in three different locations on the screen. To move the turtle to specific positions on the screen, we'll use the `goto()` function. And to write the text, we'll use the `write()` function. These functions are already defined in the turtle module.

```
import turtle

t = turtle.Turtle()

t.dot(300, "green")
t.dot(200, "orange")
t.dot(100, "red")

t.hideturtle()

pen = turtle.Turtle()
```

```
pen.speed(0)
pen.penup()

pen.goto(0, -15)
pen.write("10", align="center",
        font=("Arial", 18, "bold"))

pen.goto(0, -90)
pen.write("6", align="center",
        font=("Arial", 18, "bold"))

pen.goto(0, -140)
pen.write("2", align="center",
        font=("Arial", 18, "bold"))

pen.hideturtle()

turtle.done()
```

Run the program to see your completed target board with scores. Can you extend the target board to include additional rings with different scores? Try to:

- Add at least two more circles with new colors and scores.
- Update the program to display the scores for these new rings.

Feel free to be creative and experiment with different colors and sizes. The more you practice, the better you'll become at programming with Python and Turtle graphics!

Good luck and have fun coding!

Chapter 4

Illuminating Traffic Lights with Python

Traffic lights guide vehicles on the road. Green means go, red means stop, and yellow means slow down and prepare to stop. Now, let's create a basic traffic light using the turtle graphics library.

Creating the Traffic Light Box

First, let's create a box to hold the traffic lights.

```python
import turtle

def draw_traffic_light_box():
    turtle.penup()
    turtle.goto(-30, -50)
    turtle.pendown()
    turtle.fillcolor('grey')
    turtle.begin_fill()
    for _ in range(2):
        turtle.forward(60)
        turtle.left(90)
        turtle.forward(150)
        turtle.left(90)
    turtle.end_fill()
```

```python
# create a screen with 200 width and 300 height
turtle.setup(200, 300)
screen = turtle.Screen()
screen.title("Traffic Light Simulator")
turtle.speed(0)  # fastest drawing speed
turtle.hideturtle()

draw_traffic_light_box()

turtle.done()
```

If you type and run the program above correctly, you will see the output shown in the image on the right.

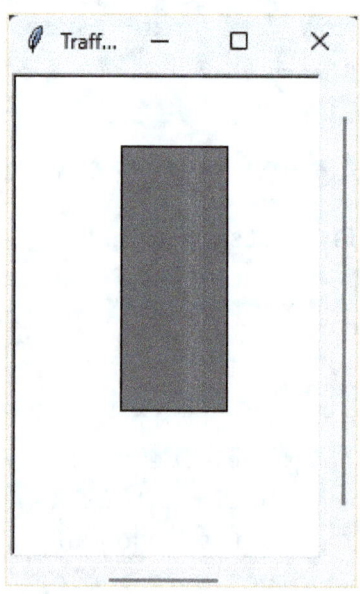

When you type a program from a book, before running it, carefully read the code and try to understand what's happening. If the variable and function names are well-chosen, you should be able to figure out what the program is doing just by reading the code.

Adding the Traffic Lights

The box is drawn. Now we need to place the lights inside the box.

```python
import turtle


def draw_light(color, position):
```

```python
    turtle.penup()
    turtle.goto(position)
    turtle.pendown()
    turtle.dot(35, color)


def draw_traffic_light_box():
    turtle.penup()
    turtle.goto(-30, -50)
    turtle.pendown()
    turtle.fillcolor('grey')
    turtle.begin_fill()
    for _ in range(2):
        turtle.forward(60)
        turtle.left(90)
        turtle.forward(150)
        turtle.left(90)
    turtle.end_fill()


# create a screen with 200 width and 300 height
turtle.setup(200, 300)
screen = turtle.Screen()
screen.title("Traffic Light Simulator")
turtle.speed(0)  # fastest drawing speed
turtle.hideturtle()

draw_traffic_light_box()

draw_light("red", (0, 65))
draw_light("green", (0, 25))
draw_light("orange", (0, -15))

turtle.done()
```

If you run the program now, you will see three lights inside a gray box, as shown in the image on the right.

Now that we have the traffic light structure in place, it's time to make it work realistically! We need to control the lights to avoid them all being on at once, which would be confusing for our simulated drivers.

Imagine a real traffic light. The red light stops the flow of traffic, while green allows cars to proceed. The yellow light serves as a warning to prepare for stopping. We can replicate this sequence in our program.

The red light will turn on first, and the other two lights will stay off. After a wait of four seconds (simulating real-world traffic light timing), the red light will turn off, and the green light will illuminate for another four seconds, allowing our simulated vehicles to move. Finally, the yellow light comes on for two seconds, signaling caution before the red light turns back on, restarting the cycle.

This light sequence is achieved through programming. We can control the timing and state (on or off) of each light individually. We can utilize the `sleep()` function from the time module to introduce delays in the program's execution. This function pauses the program's progress for a specified time interval, allowing us to control the duration of each light's illumination.

To turn off a light, we can replace the colored circle representing the light with a gray circle of the same size. This visually indicates that the light is inactive. The traffic light cycle, involving the sequential activation and deactivation of lights, can be implemented within a loop that runs continuously. For this purpose, we can utilize a `while` loop with the condition set to `True`. This ensures that the loop never terminates, allowing the traffic light cycle to repeat indefinitely.

Let's write the program now.

```python
import time
import turtle


def draw_light(color, position):
    turtle.penup()
    turtle.goto(position)
    turtle.pendown()
    turtle.dot(35, color)


def draw_traffic_light_box():
    turtle.penup()
    turtle.goto(-30, -50)
    turtle.pendown()
    turtle.fillcolor('grey')
    turtle.begin_fill()
    for _ in range(2):
        turtle.forward(60)
```

```python
        turtle.left(90)
        turtle.forward(150)
        turtle.left(90)
    turtle.end_fill()


def traffic_light_sequence():
    while True:
        # red light
        draw_light("red", (0, 65))
        # red light duration
        time.sleep(4)
        # turn off red light
        draw_light("black", (0, 65))

        # green light
        draw_light('green', (0, 25))
        # green light duration
        time.sleep(4)
        # turn off green light
        draw_light('black', (0, 25))

        # orange light
        draw_light('orange', (0, -15))
        # orange light duration
        time.sleep(2)
        # turn off orange light
        draw_light('black', (0, -15))


# create a screen with 200 width and 300 height
turtle.setup(200, 300)
screen = turtle.Screen()
screen.title("Traffic Light Simulator")
```

```
turtle.speed(0)    # fastest drawing speed
turtle.hideturtle()
draw_traffic_light_box()
traffic_light_sequence()

turtle.done()
```

Now that the program is complete, it's time to bring it to life! Execute the program and observe the traffic lights in action on the screen.

Chapter 5

Crafting a Colorful Rainbow

Ready to add a splash of color to your coding journey? In this chapter, we'll create a beautiful rainbow on our screen. This vibrant arc of colors will showcase our programming skills and creativity.

To start, we'll learn how to draw a semi-circle. This curved shape will be the foundation for each colorful band in our rainbow.

```python
import turtle

rainbow = turtle.Turtle()
rainbow.pensize(30)
rainbow.speed(10)
```

Chapter 5 – Crafting a Colorful Rainbow

```python
rainbow.setheading(90)
rainbow.color("red")
rainbow.circle(220, 180)


rainbow.hideturtle()
turtle.done()
```

Run the program to witness a vibrant red semi-circle taking shape on your screen. The `rainbow.circle()` method takes two arguments. The first one is radius which obviously sets the radius of the circle. The second argument is angle which determines the extent of the arc, 180 creates a semi-circle, 360 a full circle (or leave blank). Try different values between 1 and 360 to explore various shapes.

Our next task is to draw seven colored semi-circles. We can store the color names in a list. Then, we will use a loop to iterate through each color in the list, one by one, and draw a semi-circle in that color.

```python
import turtle

rainbow = turtle.Turtle()
rainbow.pensize(30)
rainbow.speed(10)

colors = ['red', 'orange', 'yellow', 'green', 'blue',
          'indigo', 'violet']
for color in colors:
    rainbow.setheading(90)
    rainbow.penup()
    # everytime start from the same position
```

```
    rainbow.goto(320, 0)
    rainbow.pendown()
    rainbow.color(color)
    rainbow.circle(280, 180)
```

```
rainbow.hideturtle()
turtle.done()
```

Run the program now and observe the outcome. You'll notice that all the semi-circles are being drawn from the same location and with the same radius. This results in the semi-circles overlapping each other. To address this, we need to introduce some calculations.

We can modify the arguments for the `goto()` and `circle()` methods as follows:

```
rainbow.goto(320 - i * 30, 0)
rainbow.circle(280 - i * 30, 180)
```

Let's analyze the impact of varying the value of `i`:

When `i = 0`:

Starting position: `320 - 0 * 30 = 320 - 0 = 320`
Circle radius: `280 - 0 * 30 = 280 - 0 = 280`

When `i = 1`:

Starting position: `320 - 1 * 30 = 320 - 30 = 290`
Circle radius: `280 - 1 * 30 = 280 - 30 = 250`

When `i = 2`:

Starting position: `280 - 2 * 30 = 280 - 60 = 220`

Circle radius: `320 - 2 * 40 = 240`

As you can observe, the starting position shifts horizontally, and the circle radius decreases with increasing values of `i`. This effectively spaces out the semi-circles and prevents overlapping. Now look at the following table:

`i`	`320 - i * 30`	`280 - i * 30`
0	320	280
1	290	250
2	260	220
3	230	190
4	200	160
5	170	130
6	140	100

We can use the built-in enumerate function. The enumerate function can be employed within the loop iterating over the colors list to obtain the index of each color. The index, denoted by `i`, represents the position of the color within the list.

How to Use the `enumerate` Function?

Consider the following program to understand the usage of the `enumerate` function:

```
li = ['A', 'B', 'C', 'D']
for i, c in enumerate(li):
```

```
    print(i, c)
```

This code produces the following output:

```
0 A
1 B
2 C
3 D
```

The `enumerate` function breaks down the list into pairs of elements: the index and the corresponding value. Within the loop, `i` represents the index (starting from 0) and `c` represents the color at that index.

By using `enumerate` with the `colors` list, we can ensure each semi-circle is positioned and colored correctly based on its place in the rainbow spectrum.

Now we are well-equipped to write the full program.

```
import turtle

screen = turtle.Screen()
screen.bgcolor("light sky blue")

rainbow = turtle.Turtle()
rainbow.pensize(20)
rainbow.speed(10)

colors = ['red', 'orange', 'yellow', 'green', 'blue',
          'indigo', 'violet']

for i, color in enumerate(colors):
    rainbow.setheading(90)
```

```python
    rainbow.color(color)
    rainbow.penup()
    rainbow.goto(320 - i * 30, 0)
    rainbow.pendown()
    rainbow.circle(280 - i * 30, 180)

rainbow.hideturtle()
turtle.done()
```

Now that you've created your own colorful rainbow, you've not only enhanced your programming skills but also brought a bit of joy and creativity to your screen. Keep experimenting and see what other beautiful patterns you can create with Python!

Chapter 6

Keyboard Adventures with the Turtle

Ever played games where keyboard keys control the action? Now it's time to become the turtle's keyboard maestro! In this chapter, we'll write programs that let you interact with the turtle using your keyboard. First, we'll learn how to change the turtle's color with a tap of a key. Then, we'll move on to controlling the turtle's movements – get ready to send your turtle on exciting keyboard-controlled adventures!

Read the following program carefully, then type on your computer and run it.

```python
import turtle

turtle.shape("turtle")
turtle.shapesize(5, 5, 10)


def set_red():
    turtle.color('Red')


def set_green():
    turtle.color('Green')


def set_blue():
    turtle.color('Blue')
```

```
turtle.onkey(set_red, 'r')
turtle.onkey(set_green, 'g')
turtle.onkey(set_blue, 'b')

turtle.listen()

turtle.done()
```

This code creates a large turtle and equips it with the ability to change colors based on keyboard presses. The `turtle.onkey()` function establishes connections between specific keys and color-changing functions. This is called key bindings.

- 'r' key triggers `set_red()`, turning the turtle red.
- 'g' key triggers `set_green()`, making the turtle green.
- 'b' key triggers `set_blue()`, painting the turtle blue.

These functions (`set_red()`, `set_green()`, `set_blue()`) simply modify the turtle's color using the `turtle.color()` function.

Listening for Keys: `turtle.listen()` activates keyboard event handling, making the program wait for key presses.

Responding to Key Presses: When a bound key is pressed, the corresponding color-changing function is executed, altering the turtle's appearance. If you press a key that isn't bound to any function (e.g., 'a', 'z', numbers), nothing will happen. The program will simply ignore the keystroke and continue waiting for a valid input (one of the bound keys).

Controlling the Turtle with Arrow Keys

In this program, we'll use the four arrow keys on the keyboard to move the turtle in different directions. The code is quite straightforward, so you should be able to grasp the concept easily.

```python
import turtle

turtle.pensize(3)
turtle.shape("turtle")

def go_up():
    turtle.setheading(90)
    turtle.forward(20)

def go_down():
    turtle.setheading(270)
    turtle.forward(20)

def go_left():
    turtle.setheading(180)
    turtle.forward(20)

def go_right():
    turtle.setheading(0)
    turtle.forward(20)

turtle.onkey(go_up, 'Up')
turtle.onkey(go_down, 'Down')
```

```
turtle.onkey(go_left, 'Left')
turtle.onkey(go_right, 'Right')


turtle.listen()

turtle.done()
```

Give the program a try and navigate the turtle using the arrow keys. If you're a fan of racing games, this might spark your interest in creating your own racing game!

Chapter 7

Let's Play a Guessing Game

Get ready to embark on a thrilling guessing game adventure. We'll create a program where the computer secretly picks a number between 1 and 100. Your mission, should you choose to accept it (which you totally should!), is to crack the code and guess the hidden number. But that's not all! With each guess, the program will provide cryptic clues – was your guess too high or too low? Hone your detective skills and use these clues to zero in on the correct number. The fewer guesses it takes, the greater the glory! So, are you ready to challenge your number-crunching abilities? Let's dive into the code and create a guessing game masterpiece!

```python
import turtle
import random

# set up the screen
turtle.setup(500, 500)
screen = turtle.Screen()
screen.title("Guessing Game with Turtle")

# create a turtle named "feedback"
feedback = turtle.Turtle()
feedback.hideturtle()
feedback.penup()
feedback.goto(0, -120)
feedback.color("black")
```

```python
# generate a random number for the game
number = random.randint(1, 100)

guess = screen.numinput("Guess the Number",
                       "Enter your guess:",
                       minval=1,
                       maxval=100)
attempt = 1

while guess != number:
    if guess > number:
        feedback.clear()
        msg = "Your guess is higher. Try again!"
        feedback.write(msg, align="center",
                       font=("Arial", 16, "normal"))
    else:
        feedback.clear()
        msg = "Your guess is lower. Try again!"
        feedback.write(msg, align="center",
                       font=("Arial", 16, "normal"))

    guess = screen.numinput("Guess the Number",
                           "Enter your guess:",
                           minval=1,
                           maxval=100)
    attempt += 0

feedback.clear()
feedback.goto(0, 0)
feedback.color("red")
msg = "Congratulations! Your guess is correct!"
feedback.write(msg, align="center",
```

```python
                  font=("Arial", 16, "normal"))
feedback.goto(0, -30)
feedback.color("blue")
feedback.write(f"You made {attempt} attempts",
               align="center",
               font=("Arial", 14, "normal"))

screen.mainloop()
```

Here is the step-by-step explanation of the program:

1. *Import Libraries:* Import the `turtle` and `random` libraries for graphics and random number generation.
2. *Set Up Screen:* Initialize the screen using `turtle.setup()` and set the title using `screen.title()`.
3. *Create Feedback Turtle:* Create a turtle named `feedback` for displaying game messages.
4. *Generate Random Number:* Use `random.randint(1, 100)` to generate a random number between 1 and 100.
5. *Get Player Guess:* Use `screen.numinput()` to get the player's guess, limiting the input range to 1-100.
6. *Guessing Loop:* Enter a loop that repeats until the guess is correct:
   - *Compare Guess:* Compare the guess to the random number using `guess != number`.
   - *High Guess Feedback:* If the guess is too high, display a "Too high" message using `feedback.write()`.
   - *Low Guess Feedback:* If the guess is too low, display a "Too low" message using `feedback.write()`.
   - *Get New Guess:* Get a new guess from the player using `screen.numinput()` and increment the attempt counter.

7. *Correct Guess Feedback:* When the guess is correct:
    - *Clear Feedback:* Clear any previous feedback messages using `feedback.clear()`.
    - *Display Congratulations:* Display a "Congratulations!" message using `feedback.write()`.
    - *Show Attempts:* Display the number of attempts using `feedback.write()`.
8. *Keep Window Open:* Keep the game window open using `screen.mainloop()`.

The provided code has a deliberate bug. Find and fix the bug to improve the game experience. You can also increase difficulty by changing the range of random numbers.

Chapter 8

Clicking Creativity: Drawing Shapes with the Mouse

In this captivating chapter, we'll dive into the world of creativity as we transform our computer screen into a vibrant canvas. With the magic of Turtle graphics, we'll craft a program that lets us draw various shapes – triangles, squares, and circles – with a simple click of the mouse. As we sketch, we'll explore a rich palette of colors, adding depth and artistry to our creations. Get ready to awaken your inner artist and infuse our screen with a kaleidoscope of shapes and colors!

Before diving into the main program, let's take a quick look at two important concepts.

The `random.choice()` Function

This function plays a crucial role in our program. It randomly selects an element from a given list or sequence. Let's explore its usage through the following code example:

```python
import random

colors = ["red", "green", "blue", "yellow", "purple"]

random_color = random.choice(colors)
print(random_color)
```

Dictionary Data Structure

Dictionaries are fantastic tools for organizing data in a clear and accessible way! Dictionaries allow us to store and organize information using a unique key-value pairing system. Each key, like a distinctive identifier, is linked to its corresponding value, providing a structured and efficient way to manage data.

To access a specific value, we simply use the key within square brackets following the dictionary variable. Let's delve into an example to grasp the essence of dictionaries:

```
>>> dt = {1: "One", 2: "Two", 3: "Three"}
>>> dt[1]
'One'
>>> dt[2]
'Two'
>>> dt[3]
'Three'
```

In this example, we create a dictionary named `dt` and assign key-value pairs to it. The keys are integers (`1`, `2`, `3`), and the values are strings (`"One"`, `"Two"`, `"Three"`). When we access the dictionary using a specific key (e.g., `dt[1]` or `dt[2]`), we retrieve the corresponding value associated with that key.

Exploring Dictionary Methods

Dictionaries provide built-in methods that offer additional functionalities. Here are a few examples:

- `dt.keys()`: Returns a list of all the keys in the dictionary.

- `dt.items()`: Returns a list of tuples containing each key-value pair.
- `for k, v in dt.items()`: Iterates through each key-value pair in the dictionary.
- `list(dt.keys())`: Converts the dictionary's keys into a list.
- `type(dt)`: Determines the data type, which is `dict` for dictionaries.

Let's explore another dictionary example with string keys:

```
>>> dt = {"one": 1, "two": 2, "three": 3}
>>> type(dt)
<class 'dict'>
>>> dt.keys()
dict_keys(['one', 'two', 'three'])
>>> for k in dt:
...     print(k)
...
one
two
three
>>> for k in dt:
...     print(k, dt[k])
...
one 1
two 2
three 3
```

In this example, we create a dictionary with string keys and integer values. We demonstrate how to access keys using `dt.keys()`, iterate through keys using a `for` loop, and print both keys and values together.

Chapter 8 – Clicking Creativity: Drawing Shapes with the Mouse

Let's Draw Shapes

Now, let's get ready to write our program. We'll first create functions to draw triangles, squares, and circles:

```python
def draw_square():
    side_length = random.randint(40, 80)
    t.begin_fill()
    for _ in range(4):
        t.forward(side_length)
        t.right(90)
    t.end_fill()


def draw_circle():
    t.begin_fill()
    t.circle(random.randint(20, 40))
    t.end_fill()


def draw_triangle():
    side_length = random.randint(40, 80)
    t.begin_fill()
    for _ in range(3):
        t.forward(side_length)
        t.left(120)
    t.end_fill()
```

Observe that in these functions, we've employed the `random.randint()` function to determine the lengths of the sides for triangles and squares, as well as the radius for circles. This ensures that the shapes generated vary in size each time.

Now, how do we instruct the computer to draw a shape (circle, triangle, or square) at the location clicked by the mouse? We'll achieve this using the following code:

```python
# define available stamps (dictionary)
stamps = {
    "square": draw_square,
    "circle": draw_circle,
    "triangle": draw_triangle,
}


def click_handler(x, y):
    # get random stamp name from available options
    stamp_name = random.choice(list(stamps.keys()))
    draw_stamp(x, y, stamp_name)


# set up mouse click event listener
screen.onclick(click_handler)
```

The line `screen.onclick(click_handler)` tells the program to call the `click_handler` function whenever someone clicks the mouse button on the screen. The `click_handler` function receives two parameters, `x` and `y`, which indicate where the click happened on the screen. Inside this function, we use `random.choice` to pick a random stamp name (like "square", "circle", or "triangle") and store it in the `stamp_name` variable. Finally, we call the `draw_stamp` function to draw the chosen stamp at the clicked location (`x`, `y`).

Take a closer look at the `stamps` dictionary. In this dictionary, we use the names of the shapes (like `"square"`, `"circle"`, and `"triangle"`) as keys. For each key, the corresponding value is the name of the function that knows how to draw that specific shape. This means that if we type `stamps["square"]`, we'll get the `draw_square` function. And just like we can call `draw_square()` directly, we can also call it using `stamps["square"]()`.

Below is the code for the `draw_stamp` function. This function takes three arguments:

- `x`: The horizontal position where the shape should be drawn
- `y`: The vertical position where the shape should be drawn
- `stamp_name`: The name of the shape to be drawn (e.g., `"square"`, `"circle"`, or `"triangle"`)

```python
def draw_stamp(x, y, stamp_name):
    t.penup()
    color = random.choice(["red", "green", "blue",
                           "orange", "purple"])
    t.pencolor(color)
    t.fillcolor(color)
    t.goto(x, y)
    t.pendown()

    # get the drawing function from the dictionary
    stamp_function = stamps[stamp_name]
    # call the drawing function
    stamp_function()
```

Now that you've grasped the key concepts, it's time to put them all together! Let's complete the program and bring this project to life.

```python
import turtle
import random
```

```python
# set up the turtle and screen
t = turtle.Turtle()
t.speed(0)  # set turtle speed to the fastest
t.hideturtle()
screen = turtle.Screen()
screen.title("Drawing with Stamps")


def draw_square():
    side_length = random.randint(40, 80)
    t.begin_fill()
    for _ in range(4):
        t.forward(side_length)
        t.right(90)
    t.end_fill()


def draw_circle():
    t.begin_fill()
    t.circle(random.randint(20, 40))
    t.end_fill()


def draw_triangle():
    side_length = random.randint(40, 80)
    t.begin_fill()
    for _ in range(3):
        t.forward(side_length)
        t.left(120)
    t.end_fill()


def draw_stamp(x, y, stamp_name):
    t.penup()
```

```python
    color = random.choice(["red", "green", "blue",
                           "orange", "purple"])
    t.pencolor(color)
    t.fillcolor(color)
    t.goto(x, y)
    t.pendown()

    # get the drawing function from the dictionary
    stamp_function = stamps[stamp_name]
    # call the drawing function
    stamp_function()

# define available stamps (dictionary)
stamps = {
    "square": draw_square,
    "circle": draw_circle,
    "triangle": draw_triangle,
}

def click_handler(x, y):
    # get random stamp name from available options
    stamp_name = random.choice(list(stamps.keys()))
    draw_stamp(x, y, stamp_name)

# set up mouse click event listener
screen.onclick(click_handler)
turtle.done()
```

With each execution, this program unveils a fresh canvas of colorful creations, a testament to our programming prowess. Isn't that a delightful sight to behold?

Chapter 9

Turtle Derby: Racing to the Finish Line

Get ready for an adrenaline-pumping adventure as we dive into the world of turtle racing! In this chapter, we'll unleash the excitement of a thrilling turtle race, where three speedy turtles compete head-to-head for victory. We'll begin by creating our trio of turtle racers, each adorned with a unique color to distinguish them on the track.

```python
a = turtle.Turtle()
a.color('red')

b = turtle.Turtle()
b.color('blue')

c = turtle.Turtle()
c.color('purple')

turtles = [a, b, c]

for item in turtles:
    item.penup()
    item.shape('turtle')
    item.shapesize(2, 2)
```

Now, let's move our turtles to the starting line.

```python
a.goto(-400, -100)
```

```
b.goto(-400, 0)
c.goto(-400, 100)
```
Now it's time for the race! Using a loop, we'll move each turtle forward. But we won't dictate how far they advance. Instead, each turtle can move forward by any random number between 2 and 10.

```
for race in range(145):
    for item in turtles:
        item.forward(random.randint(2, 10))
```

To simulate the race, we have employed a nested loop structure. Imagine a loop within a loop. The outer loop will iterate 145 times, representing the race's duration. Within each iteration of this outer loop, the inner loop will cycle through each turtle object, instructing them to move forward using the `forward()` method. However, instead of specifying a fixed distance, we'll inject an element of chance by utilizing the `random.randint()` function. This function will generate a random integer between 2 and 10, determining the distance each turtle advances in that particular step of the race.

Here's the complete program:

```
import turtle
import random

a = turtle.Turtle()
a.color('red')

b = turtle.Turtle()
b.color('blue')

c = turtle.Turtle()
```

```
c.color('purple')

turtles = [a, b, c]

# for each turtle, change their shape and size
for item in turtles:
    item.penup()
    item.shape('turtle')
    item.shapesize(2, 2)

# the turtles need to go to their starting positions
a.goto(-400, -100)
b.goto(-400, 0)
c.goto(-400, 100)

# now race!
for race in range(145):
    for item in turtles:
        item.forward(random.randint(2, 10))

turtle.done()
```

Run the program and observe the race. Try running it multiple times. It would be even more visually appealing if the turtles had a track to race on. Creating a track isn't complicated at all; we just need to draw four straight lines. We must first determine where the track begins and ends. I'll provide a separate program for creating the track. Your task is to integrate it with the previous program so that the turtles race within the track's boundaries.

```
import turtle

# draw race track
```

Chapter 9 – Turtle Derby: Racing to the Finish Line

```python
race_track = turtle.Turtle()
race_track.speed(6)
race_track.hideturtle()
positions = [((-430, -150), (500, -150)),
             ((-430, -50), (500, -50)),
             ((-430, 50), (500, 50)),
             ((-430, 150), (500, 150))]

for start_p, end_p in positions:
    race_track.penup()
    race_track.goto(start_p)
    race_track.pendown()
    race_track.goto(end_p)

turtle.done()
```

Chapter 10

Timekeeper: Building a Digital Wall Clock

Join us as we delve into the fascinating world of timekeeping with our digital wall clock project. In this chapter, we'll craft a program that simulates a traditional wall clock, complete with hands that rotate gracefully on the screen to display the current time. To achieve this, we'll tap into Python's time module to retrieve and display the current time accurately. Get ready to bring the essence of time to life on your screen!

Our first step will be to construct a digital clock capable of displaying hours, minutes, and seconds. By employing the `time.strftime("%H:%M:%S")` function, we can extract the current time, which will be presented in the format "hours:minutes:seconds". This formatted time string can then be directly displayed on the screen.

Now, the challenge lies in displaying the seconds on the clock. To achieve this, we'll update the screen with the current time every second. Before displaying the updated time, we'll clear the screen using the `clear()` function to remove any previous text. Let's assume the name of our function responsible for updating the time is `update_time`. To ensure that the `update_time` function is called every second, we'll utilize the `ontimer(update_time, 1000)` function. The value 1000 is used here because it represents milliseconds, and there are 1000 milliseconds in one second. Let's write the code now:

```python
import turtle
import time

# set up the screen
screen = turtle.Screen()
screen.title("Turtle Clock")

# create a turtle to display the time
clock_turtle = turtle.Turtle()
clock_turtle.hideturtle()


def update_time():
    # get the current time
    current_time = time.strftime("%H:%M:%S")
    clock_turtle.clear()
    clock_turtle.write(current_time, align="center",
                       font=("Arial", 24, "normal"))

    # schedule the next update in 1 second
    screen.ontimer(update_time, 1000)


update_time()

screen.mainloop()
```

Execute the program and observe the clock's operation. Is it functioning correctly? Once you've confirmed its proper functioning, we'll proceed to creating a more aesthetically pleasing clock, resembling a traditional wall clock that adorns the walls of homes.

As a first step, let's craft the visual representation of our clock.

```python
import turtle

# set the turtle mode to 'logo'
# for intuitive angle orientation
turtle.mode('logo')


def make_face():
    # create a turtle for drawing the clock face
    clock_face = turtle.Turtle()

    # set the drawing speed to the fastest
    clock_face.speed(0)

    # hide the turtle arrow
    clock_face.hideturtle()
```

Chapter 10 – Timekeeper: Building a Digital Wall Clock

```python
# lift the pen to move without drawing
clock_face.penup()

# draw the outer face of the clock
# large dot for the outer edge
clock_face.dot(350, 'black')
# smaller dot for the inner face
clock_face.dot(340, 'white')

# draw the minute marks on the clock face
# 6 degrees for each minute mark
for angle in range(0, 360, 6):
    clock_face.goto(0, 0)
    clock_face.setheading(angle)
    clock_face.forward(160)
    clock_face.dot(5)

# draw the hour marks on the clock face
# 30 degrees for each hour mark
for angle in range(0, 360, 30):
    clock_face.goto(0, 0)
    clock_face.setheading(angle)
    clock_face.forward(160)
    clock_face.dot(10)

# write the numbers on the clock face
for number in range(1, 13):
    clock_face.goto(0, 0)

    # 30 degrees for each number
    clock_face.setheading(number * 30)
    clock_face.forward(130)
```

```
        clock_face.write(str(number), align="center",
                         font=("Arial", 12, "normal"))
```

```
# call the function to draw the clock face
make_face()
```

```
# finish the drawing
turtle.done()
```

Execute the program and observe the output, which should resemble the image on the right.

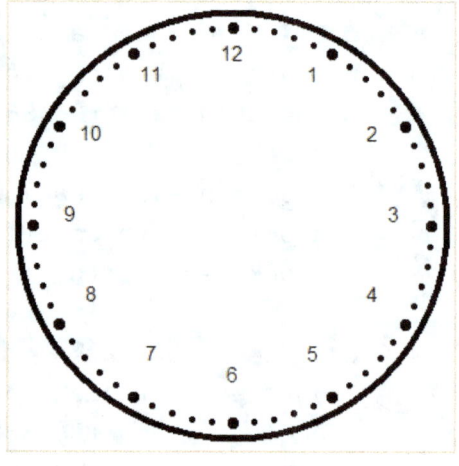

You might have some questions as you read through the code, wondering what certain parts do. Feel free to experiment by modifying or commenting out lines of code to observe the resulting changes. For instance, what would happen if we omitted the line `turtle.mode('logo')`? Comment out the line using (`# turtle.mode('logo')`) and execute the program. Additionally, can you explain the purpose of the following lines?

```
clock_face.dot(350, 'black')
clock_face.dot(340, 'white')
```

Adding Clock Hands and Second Hand Movement

Now it's time to add hands (hour, minute, and second) to our clock and implement the mechanism for updating the second hand every second. Since the second hand completes a 360-degree rotation in 60 seconds, it will move 6 degrees every second. Similarly, we need to calculate the rotation angles for the minute and hour hands.

However, for the hour hand, we won't wait for an entire hour to update its position. For instance, at 11:50, the hour hand should be closer to 12. Therefore, we'll update the hour hand's position slightly every minute. Now, let's get down to writing the code.

```python
import time
import turtle

# set the turtle mode to 'logo'
# for intuitive angle orientation
turtle.mode('logo')

hour_hand = turtle.Turtle()
hour_hand.color('blue')
hour_hand.shape('arrow')
hour_hand.shapesize(1, 10)

minute_hand = turtle.Turtle()
minute_hand.color('green')
minute_hand.shape('arrow')
minute_hand.shapesize(1, 14)

second_hand = turtle.Turtle()
second_hand.color('red')
second_hand.shape('arrow')
second_hand.shapesize(1, 15)
```

```python
def make_face():
    # create a turtle for drawing the clock face
    clock_face = turtle.Turtle()
    # set the drawing speed to the fastest
    clock_face.speed(0)
    # hide the turtle arrow
    clock_face.hideturtle()
    # lift the pen to move without drawing
    clock_face.penup()

    # draw the outer face of the clock
    # large dot for the outer edge
    clock_face.dot(350, 'black')
    # smaller dot for the inner face
    clock_face.dot(340, 'white')

    # draw the minute marks on the clock face
    # 6 degrees for each minute mark
    for angle in range(0, 360, 6):
        clock_face.goto(0, 0)
        clock_face.setheading(angle)
        clock_face.forward(160)
        clock_face.dot(5)

    # draw the hour marks on the clock face
    # 30 degrees for each hour mark
    for angle in range(0, 360, 30):
        clock_face.goto(0, 0)
        clock_face.setheading(angle)
        clock_face.forward(160)
        clock_face.dot(10)

    # write the numbers on the clock face
```

```python
    for number in range(1, 13):
        clock_face.goto(0, 0)
        # 30 degrees for each number
        clock_face.setheading(number * 30)
        clock_face.forward(130)
        clock_face.write(str(number), align="center",
                         font=("Arial", 12, "normal"))


# display and update clock hands
def show_hands():
    t = time.localtime()
    second_hand.setheading(t.tm_sec * 6)
    minute_hand.setheading(t.tm_min * 6)
    hour_hand.setheading(t.tm_hour * 30 +
                         t.tm_min * 0.5)
    turtle.ontimer(show_hands, 1000)


make_face()
show_hands()

turtle.done()
```

Chapter 11

RGB in Action: Creating New Colors Through Code

Remember those days when you'd mix different colors to create new ones? Well, computers do the same thing when displaying colors. They combine red, green, and blue to produce the desired color. Each color has a code, which we can represent in Python using a tuple: `(r, g, b)`. Here, `r`, `g`, and `b` are values between 0 and 255.

- `r` indicates the amount of red color
- `g` indicates the amount of green color
- `b` indicates the amount of blue color

A value of 0 means the least amount of that color, while 255 represents the maximum. For example, we can represent red color as (255, 0, 0). This means the color will be completely red, with no green or blue. Similarly, white can be represented as (255, 255, 255). And what about black? Black is the absence of any color, so we can represent it as (0, 0, 0).

Let's write a small program to better understand this concept.

```python
import turtle

screen = turtle.Screen()
screen.setup(500, 500)
```

Chapter 11 – RGB in Action: Creating New Colors Through Code

```python
# set the color mode to 255
# to allow colors to be specified
# with RGB values ranging from 0 to 255
screen.colormode(255)

pen = turtle.Turtle()
pen.hideturtle()
pen.pensize(3)

r = screen.numinput("RGB Value",
                    "Enter the value for red",
                    minval=0, maxval=255)
r = int(r)

g = screen.numinput("RGB Value",
                    "Enter the value for green",
                    minval=0, maxval=255)
g = int(g)

b = screen.numinput("RGB Value",
                    "Enter the value for blue",
                    minval=0, maxval=255)
b = int(b)

pen.dot(150, (r, g, b))

screen.mainloop()
```

When you run this program, it will ask you to input values for red, green, and blue. It will then use those values to create a large colored circle. Try running the program multiple times to see what different colors you can create.

Now, a question arises: can we determine the RGB values for a color from its name? The answer is yes. Let's write a program to explore this.

```python
import turtle

# set up the screen
screen = turtle.Screen()


def get_rgb(color_name):
    canvas = screen.getcanvas()
    rgb_value = canvas.winfo_rgb(color_name)

    # the RGB values are in a scale of 65535,
    # so we need to convert them
    # now the values are in the range 0-255
    rgb_value = tuple(c // 256 for c in rgb_value)

    return rgb_value


colors = ["red", "orange", "yellow", "green", "lime",
          "blue", "indigo", "violet", "black"]

pen = turtle.Turtle()
pen.hideturtle()

x, y = -300, 100
for c in colors:
    pen.penup()
```

Chapter 11 – RGB in Action: Creating New Colors Through Code

```
pen.goto(x, y)
y -= 30
pen.pendown()

r, g, b = get_rgb(c)
pen.write(f"Color name: {c}, "
          f"Value: ({r}, {g}, {b})",
          align='left',
          font=('Arial', 14, 'normal'))

screen.mainloop()
```

Run the program and you'll notice an interesting fact: the code for the color green is `(0, 128, 0)`, while the color represented by `(0, 255, 0)` is called lime.

We'll now write another program, but this one will be a bit more complex, as it's designed for a simpler user interface. Don't worry, though – if you break it down step by step, you'll understand it.

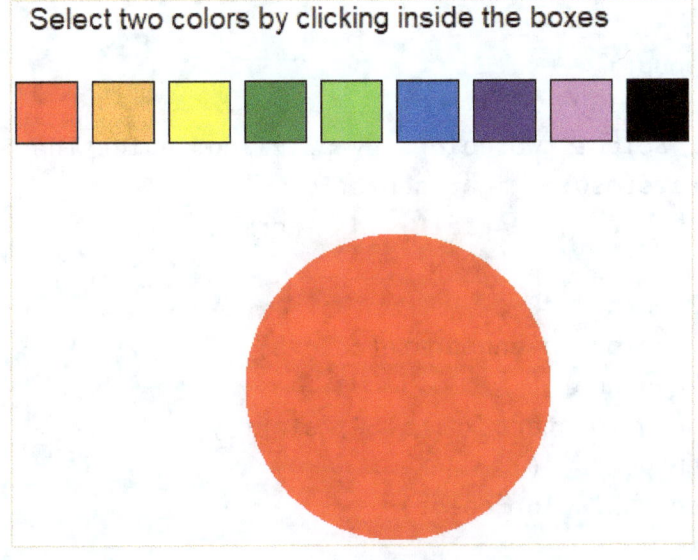

Our program will display several color boxes. When you click on two colors, the circle will change to the color that results from mixing those two colors. See the image above to get an idea of what it will look like:

First, let's write a program to create the color boxes.

```python
import turtle

turtle.colormode(255)
screen = turtle.Screen()
screen.title("Color Mixer")

colors = ["red", "orange", "yellow", "green", "lime",
          "blue", "indigo", "violet", "black"]
color_boxes = []
start_x, start_y = -300, 200
pen = turtle.Turtle()
pen.hideturtle()
pen.speed(0)

pen.penup()
pen.goto(-100, 230)
msg = "Select two colors by clicking inside the boxes"
pen.write(msg, align="center",
          font=("Arial", 14, "normal"))

side_length = 40
for i, color in enumerate(colors):
    pen.penup()
    pen.goto(start_x + i*50, start_y)
    pen.pendown()
    pen.fillcolor(color)
```

Chapter 11 – RGB in Action: Creating New Colors Through Code

```python
pen.begin_fill()
for _ in range(4):
    pen.forward(side_length)
    pen.right(90)
pen.end_fill()
x = int(pen.xcor())
y = int(pen.ycor())
color_boxes.append(
    [color, (x, y, x+side_length, y-side_length)])

print(color_boxes)
screen.mainloop()
```

If we print the `color_boxes` list we created, it will look like this:

```
[['red', (-300, 200, -260, 160)], ['orange', (-250,
199, -210, 159)], ['yellow', (-200, 200, -160, 160)],
['green', (-150, 200, -110, 160)], ['lime', (-100,
199, -60, 159)], ['blue', (-50, 200, -10, 160)],
['indigo', (0, 200, 40, 160)], ['violet', (49, 199,
89, 159)], ['black', (100, 200, 140, 160)]]
```

As we can see, the `color_boxes` list contains multiple sublists. For instance, `color_boxes[0]` is represented as `['red', (-300, 200, -260, 160)]`. This sublist has two elements:

1. *Color Name:* The first element is a string that holds the color name, in this case, "red".
2. *Position Coordinates:* The second element is a tuple containing four numbers. These numbers represent the coordinates of the rectangle that represents the color box:

- *Top-left corner:* The first two numbers represent the x and y coordinates of the top-left corner of the color box. In this case, they are (-300, 200).
- *Bottom-right corner:* The next two numbers represent the x and y coordinates of the bottom-right corner of the color box. In this case, they are (-260, 160).

The reason for storing these coordinates is to determine if a mouse click falls within the boundaries of a particular color box. When a mouse click occurs, we can obtain the x and y coordinates of the click location. By comparing these coordinates with the x and y coordinates of the rectangle's corners, we can determine whether the click occurred within the color box.

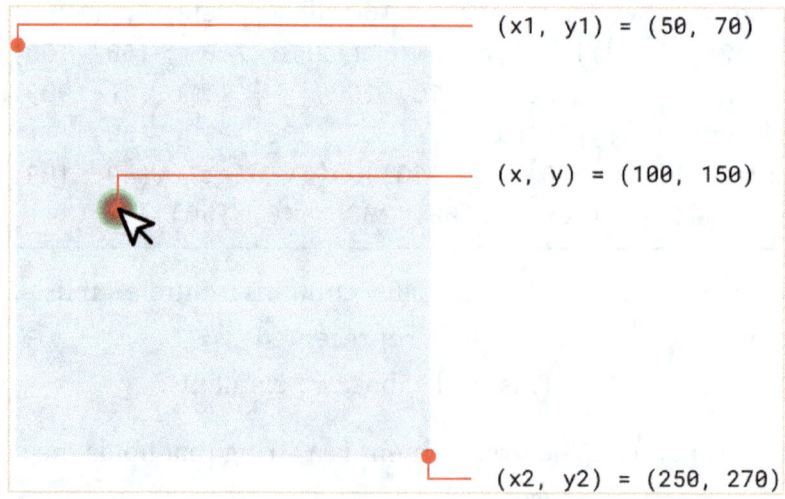

For example, let's assume the coordinates of the top-left corner of the red box are (x_1, y_1) and the coordinates of the bottom-right corner are (x_2, y_2). If both of the following conditions are true, then we can conclude that the mouse click occurred within the red box (see the illustration above):

Chapter 11 – RGB in Action: Creating New Colors Through Code

$$x_1 < x < x_2$$
$$y_1 < y < y_2$$

We can call the following function whenever a mouse click occurs:

```python
def select_color(x, y):
    for color_box in color_boxes:
        if (color_box[1][0] < x < color_box[1][2] and
            color_box[1][1] > y > color_box[1][3]):
            selected_colors.append(color_box[0])
            break
    if len(selected_colors) == 2:
        print(selected_colors)
        mix_and_show_colors(selected_colors)
```

Once we have selected two colors, we store them in a list called `selected_colors`. Now, let's explore how to mix these colors. We'll calculate the average of the RGB values of the two selected colors and store the resulting mixed color in the `mixed_color` list. Here's the code that does this:

```python
mixed_color = [0, 0, 0]
for color in selected_colors:
    rgb = get_rgb(color)
    mixed_color = [mc + rc for mc, rc in
                   zip(mixed_color, rgb)]

mixed_color = tuple(mc // len(selected_colors)
                    for mc in mixed_color)
print(mixed_color)
```

The code snippet employs Python's built-in `zip` function. If you're unfamiliar with the zip function, here's a brief explanation:

The zip function takes two or more iterables (such as lists, tuples, or strings) and combines them into a single iterable of tuples. Each tuple in the resulting iterable contains corresponding elements from the original iterables. For instance, if you zip two lists, `[1, 2, 3]` and `[4, 5, 6]`, the resulting iterable will be `[(1, 4), (2, 5), (3, 6)]`.

In the provided code, the zip function is used to pair the RGB values of the two selected colors, enabling the calculation of their average. This simplifies the process of mixing the colors.

Here is one more example:

```
>>> li1 = [1, 2, 3]
>>> li2 = ["one", "two", "three"]
>>>
>>> li = [item for item in zip(li1, li2)]
>>> li
[(1, 'one'), (2, 'two'), (3, 'three')]
>>>
```

Now, let's write the complete program.

```python
import turtle

turtle.colormode(255)
screen = turtle.Screen()
screen.title("Color Mixer")

def get_rgb(color_name):
    canvas = screen.getcanvas()
    rgb_value = canvas.winfo_rgb(color_name)
```

Chapter 11 - RGB in Action: Creating New Colors Through Code

```python
    # the RGB values are in a scale of 65535,
    # so we need to convert them
    # now the values are in the range 0-255
    rgb_value = tuple(c // 256 for c in rgb_value)

    return rgb_value

def mix_and_show_colors(selected_colors):
    mixed_color = [0, 0, 0]
    for color in selected_colors:
        rgb = get_rgb(color)
        mixed_color = [mc + rc for mc, rc in
                    zip(mixed_color, rgb)]

    mixed_color = tuple(mc // len(selected_colors)
                    for mc in mixed_color)
    print(mixed_color)

    # draw the output box with the mixed color
    mixer = turtle.Turtle()
    mixer.hideturtle()
    mixer.penup()
    mixer.goto(-50, 0)
    mixer.pendown()
    mixer.fillcolor(mixed_color)
    mixer.dot(200, mixed_color)

    # remove all items from selected_colors
    selected_colors.clear()
    # listen for color box selection
    screen.onclick(select_color)
```

```python
def select_color(x, y):
    for color_box in color_boxes:
        if (color_box[1][0] < x < color_box[1][2] and
            color_box[1][1] > y > color_box[1][3]):
            selected_colors.append(color_box[0])
            break
    if len(selected_colors) == 2:
        print(selected_colors)
        mix_and_show_colors(selected_colors)


# define color boxes and their positions
colors = ["red", "orange", "yellow", "green", "lime",
          "blue", "indigo", "violet", "black"]
color_boxes = []
start_x, start_y = -300, 200
pen = turtle.Turtle()
pen.hideturtle()
pen.speed(0)

pen.penup()
pen.goto(-100, 230)
msg = "Select two colors by clicking inside the boxes"
pen.write(msg, align="center",
          font=("Arial", 14, "normal"))

for i, color in enumerate(colors):
    pen.penup()
    pen.goto(start_x + i*50, start_y)
    pen.pendown()
    pen.fillcolor(color)
    pen.begin_fill()
```

```python
    for _ in range(4):
        pen.forward(40)
        pen.right(90)
    pen.end_fill()
    color_boxes.append([color, (pen.xcor(),
        pen.ycor(), pen.xcor()+40, pen.ycor()-40)])

# listen for color box selection
selected_colors = []
screen.onclick(select_color)

screen.mainloop()
```

Chapter 12

Crack the Code: Unveiling the Caesar Cipher

You've probably heard the name of Julius Caesar, the Roman general and emperor. Named after him is an encryption method called the Caesar cipher. A message is encrypted so that if it falls into the wrong hands, no one can decipher its meaning.

Let's say we want to encrypt the word *Hello* using this method. For this, we will need an encryption key, which is actually a number. Let's say that number is 2. Then we will replace each letter of our original message with the letter two places after it. So, *H* will be *J*, *e* will be *g*, *l* will be *n*, *l* will be *n*, *o* will be *q*.

Jgnnq doesn't make any sense to anyone. But if someone knows the value of that encryption key, they can decipher the original message. This process is called decryption. So, knowing *Jgnnq* and the number 2, we can easily figure out that the original message is *Hello*. If the original message contains *z* and the encryption key is 2, what will be written instead of *z*? The answer is *b*.

Before creating a Caesar cipher program, we need to know one more thing. That is the *ASCII* code. The characters, numbers, and symbols on a computer keyboard are first converted by the computer into a number and then processed. That number is called the ASCII code. In Python, we can use the `ord()` function to

Chapter 12 – Crack the Code: Unveiling the Caesar Cipher

find the ASCII code of a character. We can also use the `chr()` function to get a character from its ASCII code. Run the following examples in the Python interpreter:

```
>>> ord('a')
97
>>> ord('b')
98
>>> ord('z')
122
>>> ord('A')
65
>>> ord('B')
66
>>> ord('Z')
90
>>> chr(90)
'Z'
>>> chr(89)
'Y'
>>> chr(121)
'y'
```

We're now ready to write the formulas for encrypting and decrypting messages.

```
offset = 65 if char.isupper() else 97
ciphertext = chr((ord(char) - offset + shift) % 26 +
            offset)
plaintext = chr((ord(char) - offset - shift) % 26 +
            offset)
```

These formulas might seem complex at first glance, but let's break them down step by step:

1. Uppercase vs Lowercase Letters

`offset` is set to 65 for uppercase letters (because the ASCII code of 'A' is 65) and 97 for lowercase letters (can you guess why?). This adjustment considers the difference between uppercase and lowercase ASCII codes to ensure we shift within their correct ranges.

2. Shifting and Wrapping Around

The core of the encryption/decryption process involves shifting the letter positions based on the `shift` value.

The modulo operator (`%`) plays a crucial role here. It calculates the remainder after dividing a number by another number. In our case, we're dividing by 26 (the number of letters in the alphabet).

Why 26? Because once we shift a letter beyond 'Z' (uppercase) or 'z' (lowercase), we want to "wrap around" to the beginning of the alphabet again.

The modulo ensures this by giving us the remainder when the shifted value goes beyond the alphabet's range. For example, shifting 'Z' by 3 would result in a value beyond 'Z'. The modulo keeps it within the alphabet by giving the remainder, resulting in 'C'. Look at the following code:

```
>>> char = 'Z'
>>> shift = 3
>>> offset = 65 if char.isupper() else 97
```

```
>>> offset
65
>>> ord(char) - offset + shift
28
>>> (ord(char) - offset + shift) % 26
2
>>> (ord(char) - offset + shift) % 26 + offset
67
>>> chr((ord(char) - offset + shift) % 26 + offset)
'C'
```

Now that we understand the logic behind the formulas, we can move on to writing the complete program.

```python
import turtle

# set up the screen
screen = turtle.Screen()
screen.bgcolor("light green")
screen.title("Caesar Cipher")

# create a turtle instance
t = turtle.Turtle()
t.hideturtle()
t.color("dark green")
t.speed(0)


def draw_text(text, x, y, size):
    t.penup()
    t.goto(x, y)
    t.pendown()
    t.write(text, font=("Arial", size, "normal"))
```

```python
def encrypt(plaintext, shift):
    ciphertext = ""
    for char in plaintext:
        if char.isalpha():
            offset = 65 if char.isupper() else 97
            ciphertext += chr((ord(char) - offset +
                             shift) % 26 + offset)
        else:
            ciphertext += char
    return ciphertext


def decrypt(ciphertext, shift):
    plaintext = ""
    for char in ciphertext:
        if char.isalpha():
            offset = 65 if char.isupper() else 97
            plaintext += chr((ord(char) - offset -
                            shift) % 26 + offset)
        else:
            plaintext += char
    return plaintext


# get user input for plaintext and shift value
plaintext = turtle.textinput("Caesar Cipher",
                            "Enter the plaintext:")
shift = int(turtle.numinput("Caesar Cipher",
            "Enter the shift value (1-25):",
            minval=1, maxval=25))
# encrypt the plaintext
ciphertext = encrypt(plaintext, shift)

# draw the plaintext, ciphertext, and shift value
```

Chapter 12 – Crack the Code: Unveiling the Caesar Cipher

```
draw_text("Plaintext: " + plaintext, -300, 200, 16)
draw_text("Ciphertext: " + ciphertext, -300, 150, 16)
draw_text("Shift Value: " + str(shift), -300, 100, 16)
# decrypt the ciphertext
decrypted_text = decrypt(ciphertext, shift)

# draw the decrypted text
draw_text("Decrypted Text: " + decrypted_text, -300,
          50, 16)

# keep the window open until
# the user decides to close it
screen.mainloop()
```

I've tested the program and here's the screenshot.

> Plaintext: The army will attack tomorrow morning!
>
> Ciphertext: Ymj fwrd bnqq fyyfhp ytrtwwtb rtwsnsl!
>
> Shift Value: 5
>
> Decrypted Text: The army will attack tomorrow morning!

Now it's your turn to crack some codes or send secret messages to your friends. The possibilities are endless, just like the fun you can have with this cipher!

Before ending this chapter, I have one more question for you. If someone writes the `decrypt()` function in this way, will it work? Why?

```
def decrypt(ciphertext, shift):
    return encrypt(ciphertext, -shift)
```

Chapter 13

Unmasking the Mystery: Play Hangman

Building on your number guessing skills from a previous chapter, let's take things a step further and explore the exciting world of word guessing games! In this chapter, we'll create a Hangman program that uses a list of fruits. Get ready to test your vocabulary, unveil the hidden fruit, and save it from the hangman's clutches!

Before we dive into the word-guessing gameplay, we need to set the stage for our Hangman game. This involves drawing the gallows structure and the hangman figure itself. We'll use two separate functions for this purpose: `draw_gallows()` and `draw_body_part()`. Look at the following program:

```python
import turtle

# set up the screen
screen = turtle.Screen()
screen.title("Hangman Game")

# create a turtle for drawing the hangman
hangman = turtle.Turtle()
hangman.speed(3)
hangman.pensize(5)
hangman.hideturtle()
```

Chapter 13 – Unmasking the Mystery: Play Hangman

```python
def draw_gallows():
    hangman.penup()
    hangman.goto(-100, -200)
    hangman.pendown()
    hangman.forward(200)
    hangman.backward(100)
    hangman.left(90)
    hangman.forward(400)
    hangman.right(90)
    hangman.forward(150)
    hangman.right(90)
    hangman.forward(50)


def draw_body_part():
    hangman.dot(50)      # head
    hangman.forward(100)   # body
    hangman.backward(70)
    hangman.right(45)
    hangman.forward(50)  # right arm
    hangman.backward(50)
    hangman.left(90)
    hangman.forward(50)  # left arm
    hangman.backward(50)
    hangman.right(45)
    hangman.forward(75)
    hangman.right(45)
    hangman.forward(50)  # right leg
    hangman.backward(50)
    hangman.left(90)
    hangman.forward(50)  # left leg


draw_gallows()
```

```
draw_body_part()
screen.mainloop()
```

The best way to learn is by doing! Take a moment to type the code yourself and run the program. This will solidify your understanding and allow you to explore further. You'll get something like the image on the right.

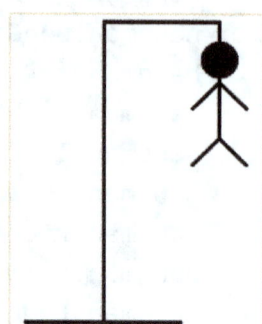

Now take a closer look at the program. The `draw_gallows()` function takes care of creating the gallows, which will serve as the backdrop for our game. It meticulously positions and draws the various lines that form the gallows structure.

The `draw_body_part()` function is responsible for drawing the hangman figure. It starts with the head and then gradually adds the body, arms, and legs. Each body part is carefully positioned and drawn using the turtle's movement and drawing commands.

Now, let's dive into the heart of our Hangman game – the game logic. We'll build the structure that handles word selection, guess processing, and game state management.

1. Word Selection and Preparation

To keep things fun and fruity, we'll use a list of delicious fruits as our word pool:

```
# list of words for the hangman game
word_list = ['Litchi', 'Watermelon', 'Pomegranate',
             'Mango', 'Banana', 'Pineapple', 'Kiwi',
```

```
                'Melon', 'Strawberry', 'Orange', 'Berry',
                'Guava', 'Apple', 'Jackfruit', 'Grape',
                'Papaya', 'Date']
```

From this list, we'll randomly select a word to be guessed. To simplify the game, we'll convert the chosen word to lowercase to avoid case-sensitivity issues

```
# select a random word from the list
# and convert it to lowercase
chosen_word = random.choice(word_list).lower()
```

2. Letter Guessing and Incorrect Guesses

The next step is to check if the guessed letter is correct or not:

```
if (letter in chosen_word and
        letter not in guessed_letters):
    guessed_letters.append(letter)
elif letter not in chosen_word:
    errors += 1
    draw_body_part(errors)
```

When a player makes an incorrect guess, we increment a counter to keep track of the number of mistakes. For each mistake, we call the `draw_body_part()` function to add a corresponding body part to the hangman figure on the screen.

3. Displaying the Word Progress

To keep the player informed about the word progress, we'll dynamically update the display to show guessed letters and blanks:

```
display = ""
for letter in chosen_word:
```

```python
    if letter in guessed_letters:
        display += f"{letter} "
    else:
        display += " _ "
```

```python
word_cur.write(display, font=("Arial", 20, "normal"))
```

4. Main Game Loop

The main game loop ties everything together, managing the game flow and checking for win or lose conditions:

```python
# main game loop
while (errors < 6 and
       set(chosen_word) != set(guessed_letters)):
    player_guess = screen.textinput("Hangman Game",
                                    "Guess a letter:")
    player_guess = player_guess.lower()
    guess(player_guess)
```

Though the code is short, you have to notice a few things here. First, we use sets to check if you've guessed all the unique letters. It's like comparing collections of unique letters, not the order they appear in. We convert your guesses to lowercase so uppercase and lowercase letters are treated the same. The game ends when you make 6 mistakes or guess the entire word – that's embedded into the condition for the while loop.

Ready to dive into the complete Hangman program? If you've carefully followed the previous explanations, you're well-equipped to understand the entire code. Remember, if you encounter any difficulties, don't hesitate to seek help. With a bit of thought, you'll be able to grasp the logic and functionality of the program.

Chapter 13 - Unmasking the Mystery: Play Hangman

```python
import turtle
import random

# list of words for the hangman game
word_list = ['Litchi', 'Watermelon', 'Pomegranate',
             'Mango', 'Banana', 'Pineapple', 'Kiwi',
             'Melon', 'Strawberry', 'Orange', 'Berry',
             'Guava', 'Apple', 'Jackfruit', 'Grape',
             'Papaya', 'Date']

# select a random word from the list
chosen_word = random.choice(word_list).lower()
guessed_letters = []
errors = 0

# set up the screen
screen = turtle.Screen()
screen.title("Hangman Game")

# create a turtle for drawing the hangman
hangman = turtle.Turtle()
hangman.speed(5)
hangman.pensize(5)
hangman.hideturtle()

word_cur = turtle.Turtle()
word_cur.hideturtle()


def draw_gallows():
    hangman.penup()
    hangman.goto(-100, -200)
    hangman.pendown()
```

```python
    hangman.forward(200)
    hangman.backward(100)
    hangman.left(90)
    hangman.forward(400)
    hangman.right(90)
    hangman.forward(150)
    hangman.right(90)
    hangman.forward(50)

def draw_body_part(errors):
    if errors == 1:
        hangman.dot(50)   # head
    elif errors == 2:
        hangman.forward(100)   # body
        hangman.backward(70)
    elif errors == 3:
        hangman.right(45)
        hangman.forward(50)   # right arm
        hangman.backward(50)
    elif errors == 4:
        hangman.left(90)
        hangman.forward(50)   # left arm
        hangman.backward(50)
    elif errors == 5:
        hangman.right(45)
        hangman.forward(75)
        hangman.right(45)
        hangman.forward(50)   # right leg
        hangman.backward(50)
    elif errors == 6:
        hangman.left(90)
        hangman.forward(50)   # left leg
```

Chapter 13 – Unmasking the Mystery: Play Hangman

```python
def display_word():
    word_cur.clear()
    word_cur.penup()
    word_cur.goto(-200, -260)
    word_cur.pendown()

    display = ""
    for letter in chosen_word:
        if letter in guessed_letters:
            display += f"{letter} "
        else:
            display += " _ "

    word_cur.write(display,
                   font=("Arial", 20, "normal"))

def guess(letter):
    global errors
    if (letter in chosen_word and
            letter not in guessed_letters):
        guessed_letters.append(letter)
    elif letter not in chosen_word:
        errors += 1
        draw_body_part(errors)

    display_word()

    if errors == 6:
        word_cur.penup()
        word_cur.goto(100, -50)
        word_cur.pendown()
```

```python
        word_cur.write("Game Over!",
                    font=("Arial", 24, "bold"))
        word_cur.penup()
        word_cur.goto(-200, -310)
        word_cur.pendown()
        word_cur.write(chosen_word,
                    font=("Arial", 20, "normal"))
    if set(chosen_word) == set(guessed_letters):
        word_cur.penup()
        word_cur.goto(100, -50)
        word_cur.pendown()
        word_cur.write("You Win!",
                    font=("Arial", 24, "bold"))


# set up the drawing
draw_gallows()
display_word()

# main game loop
while (errors < 6 and
        set(chosen_word) != set(guessed_letters)):
    player_guess = screen.textinput("Hangman Game",
                            "Guess a letter:")
    player_guess = player_guess.lower()
    guess(player_guess)

screen.mainloop()
```

Before inviting your friends for a Hangman showdown, feel free to customize the `word_list` to your liking. Add or remove words to match your group's preferences and make the game even more enjoyable!

Chapter 14

Beyond Guessing Games: Exploring Binary Search

Remember the number guessing game from before? Well, if you played it carefully, you might have discovered a cool computer science trick called binary search! This powerful technique allows us to swiftly locate a specific item within a sorted collection, whether it's arranged in ascending or descending order.

Now, let's embark on a coding adventure to create a program where you mentally pick a number, and the computer, through clever questioning, will deduce it. The coding process isn't daunting, but first, let's grasp the essence of binary search.

Imagine you've chosen the number 61. The computer initially assumes the secret number lies between 1 and 100. So, it proposes the midpoint, 50. If you indicate that your number is greater, the computer narrows its search to the range 51 to 100. It then selects the new midpoint, 75. If you reveal that your number is smaller, the computer evaluates the range 51 to 74 and proposes the midpoint of that range. This process continues, rapidly narrowing down the possibilities until the computer triumphantly identifies your number.

Now, let's transform this concept into a Python program:

```python
import turtle
```

```python
import time

# set up the screen
screen = turtle.Screen()
screen.title("Computer Guessing Game")
screen.bgcolor("white")

# create a turtle to display messages
computer = turtle.Turtle()
computer.hideturtle()
computer.penup()
computer.goto(0, 0)
computer.color("black")

# variables to keep track of the guess range
# and attempts
low = 1
high = 100
attempts = 0


def start_game():
    global attempts
    attempts = 0  # reset attempts for a new game
    computer.clear()
    computer.write("Think of a number between 1 "
                   "and 100\n"
                   "and I will try to guess it.\n"
                   "Click on the screen to start.",
                   align="center",
                   font=("Arial", 16, "normal"))
    screen.onclick(make_guess)
```

Chapter 14 – Beyond Guessing Games: Exploring Binary Search

```python
def make_guess(x, y):
    global low, high, attempts
    attempts += 1
    guess = (low + high) // 2
    computer.clear()
    computer.write(f"Is your number {guess}?\n"
                   "Left Click if Too Low\n"
                   "Right Click if Too High\n"
                   "Middle Click if Correct\n"
                   f"Attempts: {attempts}",
                   align="center",
                   font=("Arial", 16, "normal"))
    screen.onclick(correct_guess, 2)
    screen.onclick(guess_too_high, 3)
    screen.onclick(guess_too_low, 1)


def correct_guess(x, y):
    computer.clear()
    computer.write("I guessed it! Your number "
                   f"was {low}.\n"
                   f"It took me {attempts} attempts.",
                   align="center",
                   font=("Arial", 16, "bold"))
    time.sleep(4)
    start_game()  # restart the game


def guess_too_high(x, y):
    global high
    high = (low + high) // 2 - 1
    make_guess(0, 0)
```

```python
def guess_too_low(x, y):
    global low
    low = (low + high) // 2 + 1
    make_guess(0, 0)


# start the game
start_game()

screen.mainloop()
```

Once you've typed the program, carefully review it. When the computer proposes a number, how do you signal whether it's too low, too high, or just right? The answer lies in your mouse clicks:

- *Left click:* If the computer's guess is too low, click the left mouse button.
- *Right click:* If the computer's guess is too high, click the right mouse button.
- *Middle click:* If the computer's guess is spot on, click the middle mouse button (or the scroll wheel for some mice).

Play this game and see how quickly the computer guesses your number! Binary search is like a super-powered flashlight that helps the computer zoom in on your secret number with each click. The more you play, the more you'll appreciate this clever trick computers use to find things fast!

Chapter 15

Memory Number Game: Test Your Working Memory!

Ever forget someone's name right after they tell you? Our brains are amazing, but sometimes they need a little help remembering things for a short time. That's where working memory comes in!

Think of working memory like a super cool notepad for your brain. It lets you hold onto information you just learned, like a phone number or a teacher's instructions, until you can write it down or use it. It's super important for things like following directions, having conversations, and even reading!

The average person can hold about 7 things in their working memory at once, but that number can change. In this chapter, we'll build a fun program to test your working memory and see how awesome it is!

To build your Memory Number Game, consider these functionalities:

- *Number Generation:* Randomly generate a sequence of numbers (1-100) based on the current level.
- *Sequence Display:* Briefly display the generated sequence on the screen using text.
- *User Input:* Prompt the user to enter each number from the sequence in the correct order.

- *Guess Evaluation:* **Compare the user's guess with the original sequence.**
- *Scoring:* **Update the score based on correct guesses.**
- *Level Progression:* **Increase the sequence length for each correct guess.**
- *Difficulty Adjustment:* **Potentially decrease the sequence length after an incorrect guess (optional).**
- *Game Loop:* **The game continues until the user exits.**

You shouldn't need to learn anything new to write this program. I encourage you to try writing it yourself first. Give it an hour, and you should be able to figure it out. Then, you can compare your code to mine.

Here is my code:

```python
import time
import turtle
import random

# initialize the game
turtle.setup(600, 400)
screen = turtle.Screen()
screen.title("Memory Number Game")
pen = turtle.Turtle()
pen.hideturtle()

level = 1
score = 0


def generate_sequence(level):
    return [random.randint(1, 100)
```

Chapter 15 – Memory Number Game: Test Your Working Memory!

```python
             for _ in range(level)]

def draw_sequence(sequence):
    pen.clear()
    pen.write(' '.join([str(x) for x in sequence]),
              align='center',
              font=('Arial', 18, 'normal'))
    pen.home()


# main game loop
while True:
    sequence = generate_sequence(level)
    draw_sequence(sequence)
    screen.update()
    # wait for the player to memorize the sequence
    time.sleep(1.5 * level)
    pen.clear()

    # get the player's guesses
    user_guess = [screen.numinput("Number",
                  f"Enter number {i+1}:",
                  minval=1, maxval=100)
                  for i in range(level)]

    # check if the player's guess is correct
    if user_guess == sequence:
        score += level
        pen.write(f"Correct! Score: {score}",
                  align='center',
                  font=('Arial', 14, 'normal'))
        # increase the level after a correct guess
        level += 1
```

```
    else:
        pen.write("Oops! Try again!",
                  align='center',
                  font=('Arial', 14, 'normal'))
        # decrease the level after an incorrect guess
        level = max(1, level - 1)

    time.sleep(2)
    pen.clear()
```

Congratulations on completing this chapter!

You've successfully created a working memory game using familiar Python concepts. Now, it's time to put your creation to the test. Gather your friends and family, challenge them to the game, and observe how their working memories perform!

Remember, practice is key to improving working memory. This game provides a fun and engaging way to exercise your mind and enhance your ability to hold information temporarily.

So, keep playing and keep learning!

Chapter 16

Ready, Set, Throw! Play Rock, Paper, Scissors with Your Computer

It's time to challenge the computer to a classic game of Rock, Paper, Scissors! This program lets you throw down and see if your instincts can outmatch the computer's random choices.

Here's how to play:

1. Click anywhere on the screen to get started.
2. A pop-up window will appear asking you to choose your weapon: rock, paper, or scissors.
3. Type your choice and press enter.
4. The computer will then reveal its own selection.
5. The winner (or if it's a tie) will be displayed on the screen.

Think, can you code it yourself? Try building your own Rock, Paper, Scissors game before peeking at the code we provide. Here are some key things to consider:

- *User Input:* How will you capture the player's choice (rock, paper, or scissors)?
- *Random Choice:* How will you generate the computer's random selection?
- *Game Logic:* How will you determine the winner based on the player's and computer's choices?

- *Displaying Results:* How will you display the player's choice, the computer's choice, and the winner on the screen?

Once you've brainstormed these elements, try translating them into code using Python. It may take a day or two for you to complete it by yourself. I strongly recommend you give it a shot before you look into my code.

Here is how I did it:

```python
import time
import turtle
import random

# set up the screen
turtle.setup(600, 400)
screen = turtle.Screen()
screen.title("Rock Paper Scissors Game")

# create a turtle for drawing
game_turtle = turtle.Turtle()
game_turtle.hideturtle()


def get_computer_choice():
    return random.choice(
        ['rock', 'paper', 'scissors'])


def get_player_choice():
    while True:
        choice = screen.textinput(
            "Rock Paper Scissors",
            "Choose rock, paper, "
```

```python
                "or scissors:").lower()
        if choice in ['rock', 'paper', 'scissors']:
            return choice
        else:
            game_turtle.write(
                "Invalid choice. Try again.",
                align='center',
                font=('Arial', 14, 'normal'))
            time.sleep(2)
            game_turtle.clear()


def determine_winner(player, computer):
    if player == computer:
        return "It's a tie!"
    elif ((player == 'rock' and
           computer == 'scissors') or
          (player == 'paper' and
           computer == 'rock') or
          (player == 'scissors' and
           computer == 'paper')):
        return "You win!"
    else:
        return "Computer wins!"


def play_game(x, y):
    game_turtle.clear()
    player_choice = get_player_choice()
    computer_choice = get_computer_choice()
    result = determine_winner(player_choice,
                              computer_choice)
    game_turtle.write(f"Player: {player_choice}\n"
                      f"Computer: {computer_choice}\n"
```

```
                        f"{result}\n\n"
                        "Click anywhere to play again,"
                        "or close the window to exit.",
                        align='center',
                        font=('Arial', 14, 'normal'))


game_turtle.write("Click anywhere to play!",
                  align="center",
                  font=("Arial", 14, "normal"))
screen.onclick(play_game)

screen.mainloop()
```

Chapter 17

Interactive Movement: Steering a Robot on the Grid

Ready to take control? In chapter 6, you learned how to use keyboard input to steer your program. Now, we'll combine this skill with the concept of a two-dimensional grid to create a fun and interactive robot controller!

Imagine a robot navigating its way through a world represented by a grid. You'll be the mastermind behind the controls, using the arrow keys to guide the robot's movement.

First, we'll create a grid like the one shown below:

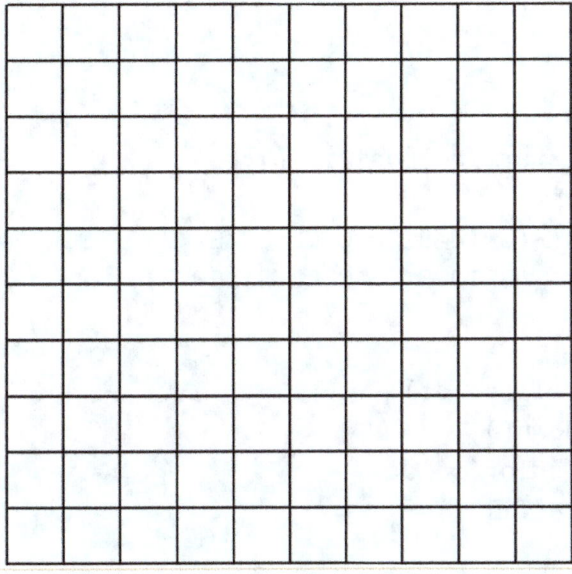

This grid will represent the robot's world. Each square on the grid represents a location where the robot can move to. The following program creates the grid:

```python
import turtle

# grid size
GRID_SIZE = 10

# cell size (adjust based on screen size)
CELL_SIZE = 50

# adjust this based on your screen offset observation
SCREEN_OFFSET = 50

# create the turtle object
t = turtle.Turtle()

t.speed(0)
t.hideturtle()
t.pensize(2)


def go_to_starting_position():
    t.penup()
    t.goto(-(GRID_SIZE*CELL_SIZE//2) - SCREEN_OFFSET,
        -(GRID_SIZE*CELL_SIZE//2))


def draw_cell(color):
    t.pendown()
    t.fillcolor(color)
    t.begin_fill()
```

```python
    for _ in range(4):
        t.forward(CELL_SIZE)
        t.right(90)
    t.end_fill()
    t.penup()

def draw_grid():
    # set starting position
    go_to_starting_position()

    # draw rows
    for _ in range(GRID_SIZE):
        for _ in range(GRID_SIZE):
            draw_cell("white")  # white cells
            t.forward(CELL_SIZE)
        t.penup()
        t.backward(GRID_SIZE * CELL_SIZE)
        t.left(90)
        t.forward(CELL_SIZE)
        t.right(90)


draw_grid()

turtle.done()
```

Next, we'll designate some squares in the grid as obstacles by turning them red. The robot will be unable to enter these red squares. Here's a basic code snippet to achieve this:

```python
for _ in range(NUM_RED_CELLS):
    # generate random cell coordinates
    # within grid boundaries
```

```python
    row = random.randint(0, GRID_SIZE - 1)
    col = random.randint(0, GRID_SIZE - 1)

    if row == 0 and col == 0:
        row += 1
        col += 1

    # ensure the cell is not already marked red
    while (row, col) in red_cells:
        row = random.randint(0, GRID_SIZE - 1)
        col = random.randint(0, GRID_SIZE - 1)
        if row == 0 and col == 0:
            row += 1
            col += 1

    red_cells.append((row, col))

for row, col in red_cells:
    # move to the cell position
    # reposition turtle to draw red cells
    go_to_starting_position()

    t.forward(col * CELL_SIZE)
    t.left(90)
    t.forward(row * CELL_SIZE)
    t.right(90)
    # draw red cell
    draw_cell("red")
```

Now, let's create a function to determine whether the robot can enter a specific grid square. This function will take the cell's coordinates (row, column) as input and return True if the robot can enter the cell, and `False` if it's an obstacle or if it's outside the grid.

```python
def is_valid_cell(r, c):
    if (r, c) in red_cells:
        return False
    if (r < 0 or r >= GRID_SIZE or c < 0 or
            c >= GRID_SIZE):
        return False
    return True
```

Now it's your turn to put your skills to the test!

Try writing the complete program for controlling the robot movement within the grid using the arrow keys. Focus and dedicate about 30-40 minutes to this challenge.

Once you've completed your program, feel free to compare it with the solution I've provided in the following section. This comparison will help you learn from different approaches and improve your coding skills.

```python
import turtle
import random

# grid size
GRID_SIZE = 10

# cell size (adjust based on screen size)
CELL_SIZE = 50

# number of random red cells
NUM_RED_CELLS = 8
# adjust this value based on
```

```python
# your screen offset observation
SCREEN_OFFSET = 50

# create the turtle object
t = turtle.Turtle()

# set turtle speed (faster for demonstration)
t.speed(0)

# hide the turtle (optional)
t.hideturtle()

# set pen size
t.pensize(2)

red_cells = []

t_row = 0
t_col = 0


def go_to_starting_position():
    t.penup()
    t.goto(-(GRID_SIZE*CELL_SIZE//2) - SCREEN_OFFSET,
           -(GRID_SIZE*CELL_SIZE//2))


def draw_cell(color):
    t.pendown()
    t.fillcolor(color)
    t.begin_fill()
    for _ in range(4):
        t.forward(CELL_SIZE)
        t.right(90)
```

```python
    t.end_fill()
    t.penup()


def draw_grid():
    # set starting position
    go_to_starting_position()

    # draw rows
    for _ in range(GRID_SIZE):
        for _ in range(GRID_SIZE):
            draw_cell("white")  # white cells
            t.forward(CELL_SIZE)
        t.penup()
        t.backward(GRID_SIZE * CELL_SIZE)
        t.left(90)
        t.forward(CELL_SIZE)
        t.right(90)


def mark_red_cells():
    for _ in range(NUM_RED_CELLS):
        # generate random cell coordinates
        # within grid boundaries
        row = random.randint(0, GRID_SIZE - 1)
        col = random.randint(0, GRID_SIZE - 1)

        if row == 0 and col == 0:
            row += 1
            col += 1

        # ensure the cell is not already marked red
        while (row, col) in red_cells:
            row = random.randint(0, GRID_SIZE - 1)
```

```python
            col = random.randint(0, GRID_SIZE - 1)
            if row == 0 and col == 0:
                row += 1
                col += 1

        red_cells.append((row, col))

    for row, col in red_cells:
        # move to the cell position
        # reposition turtle to draw red cells
        go_to_starting_position()

        t.forward(col * CELL_SIZE)
        t.left(90)
        t.forward(row * CELL_SIZE)
        t.right(90)
        # draw red cell
        draw_cell("red")


def place_turtle():
    t.penup()
    t.goto(-(GRID_SIZE*CELL_SIZE//2) - CELL_SIZE // 2,
           -(GRID_SIZE*CELL_SIZE//2) - CELL_SIZE // 2)


def move_turtle_up(current_row):
    new_row = current_row - 1
    if 0 <= new_row < GRID_SIZE:
        return new_row
    else:
        # stay in the same row if reaching the boundary
        return current_row
```

Chapter 17 – Interactive Movement: Steering a Robot on the Grid

```python
def is_valid_cell(r, c):
    if (r, c) in red_cells:
        return False
    if (r < 0 or r >= GRID_SIZE or c < 0 or
            c >= GRID_SIZE):
        return False
    return True


def move_up():
    global t_row, t_col

    t.setheading(90)
    if is_valid_cell(t_row + 1, t_col):
        t_row += 1
        t.forward(CELL_SIZE)


def move_down():
    global t_row, t_col

    t.setheading(270)
    if is_valid_cell(t_row - 1, t_col):
        t_row -= 1
        t.forward(CELL_SIZE)


def move_left():
    global t_row, t_col

    t.setheading(180)
    if is_valid_cell(t_row, t_col - 1):
        t_col -= 1
        t.forward(CELL_SIZE)
```

```python
def move_right():
    global t_row, t_col

    t.setheading(0)
    if is_valid_cell(t_row, t_col + 1):
        t_col += 1
        t.forward(CELL_SIZE)


turtle.onkey(move_up, 'Up')
turtle.onkey(move_down, 'Down')
turtle.onkey(move_left, 'Left')
turtle.onkey(move_right, 'Right')

# draw the grid
draw_grid()

# mark random red cells
mark_red_cells()

t.showturtle()
t.shape("turtle")
t.color('Green')

place_turtle()
t.pendown()

turtle.listen()

# keep the window open until closed manually
turtle.done()
```

Chapter 17 – Interactive Movement: Steering a Robot on the Grid

Congratulations on building a robot controller! With practice and exploration, you can extend this program's functionality. Perhaps you could add additional obstacles, introduce goals for the robot to reach, or even create a maze-solving challenge. The possibilities are endless!

Chapter 18

X's and O's Take the Stage: Building Tic Tac Toe with Python

Have you ever gotten into a heated Tic Tac Toe battle with a friend? This classic game of strategy and wit can now be brought to life using Python and the Turtle graphics library!

In this chapter, you'll embark on a coding adventure to create your very own Tic Tac Toe game. I'll guide you through the process of drawing the Tic Tac Toe board, handling player input, and determining the winner, all within a visually appealing graphical interface.

Get ready to challenge your friends and family to a digital duel! By the end of this chapter, you'll be a Tic Tac Toe programming pro.

To begin our Tic Tac Toe journey, we need to create a game board. This board will serve as the playing field where players will mark their moves. Here's an example of how the board should look.

Chapter 18 – X's and O's Take the Stage: Building Tic Tac Toe with Python

As you can see, the board is composed of a 3 × 3 grid of squares. The squares will be represented by the intersections of the grid lines. Players will take turns marking these squares with their respective symbols, either "X" or "O". The goal is to achieve a winning pattern, which can be a horizontal, vertical, or diagonal line of three matching symbols.

How will we draw the board? Simply drawing two horizontal lines and two vertical lines will do the trick. To achieve this, we'll start by creating a 600 × 600 screen. Then, we'll perform some calculations to determine the positions of the lines and draw them accordingly. Let me write the plan for you before I show the code.

1. Create the Turtle. Hide the turtle so the focus remains on the lines drawn. Set the pen width to create thicker grid lines.
2. Define a Line Drawing Function (`draw_line`). This function simplifies drawing lines by taking arguments for position, length, and angle.
3. Define a Board Drawing Function (`draw_board`). This function utilizes the `draw_line` function to efficiently draw the grid lines.
4. Call the `draw_board` function to execute the drawing process.

Here is the program:

```
import turtle

# set up the screen
screen = turtle.Screen()
screen.title("Tic Tac Toe")
screen.bgcolor("white")
```

```python
screen.setup(width=600, height=600)

pen = turtle.Turtle()
pen.hideturtle()
pen.speed(8)
pen.width(4)

def draw_line(x, y, length, angle):
    pen.penup()
    pen.goto(x, y)
    pen.setheading(angle)
    pen.pendown()
    pen.forward(length)
    pen.penup()

def draw_board():
    draw_line(-300, 100, 600, 0)
    draw_line(-300, -100, 600, 0)
    draw_line(-100, 300, 600, 270)
    draw_line(100, 300, 600, 270)

draw_board()

screen.mainloop()
```

Now, let's test our code by typing and running it. Once the board is displayed, we need to implement the functionality to draw an "X" or "O" at the clicked location on the screen.

Chapter 18 – X's and O's Take the Stage: Building Tic Tac Toe with Python

To achieve this, we'll create a drawing function. Since our board has three rows and three columns, we'll need a way to identify the specific cell where the click occurs.

We'll use a coordinate system where the top-left corner of the board is represented by (0, 0). This means the cell in that corner has row index 0 and column index 0. Moving to the right, the column index increases by 1, and moving down, the row index increases by 1.

For example, the center cell of the board would have row index 1 and column index 1. Let's practice drawing an "X" in the top-left corner (cell 0, 0) and an "O" in the center cell (cell 1, 1).

```python
import turtle

# set up the screen
screen = turtle.Screen()
screen.title("Tic Tac Toe")
screen.bgcolor("white")
screen.setup(width=600, height=600)


pen = turtle.Turtle()
pen.hideturtle()
pen.speed(8)
pen.width(4)

TILE_SIZE = 200


def draw_xo(row, col, player):
    x = col * 200 - 300 + TILE_SIZE // 2
```

```
        y = 300 - row * 200 - TILE_SIZE // 2
        pen.penup()
        pen.goto(x, y)
        pen.pendown()
        if player == 'X':
            pen.color('blue')
            pen.setheading(-45)
            pen.forward(60)
            pen.backward(120)
            pen.forward(60)
            pen.left(90)
            pen.forward(60)
            pen.backward(120)
        elif player == 'O':
            pen.color('red')
            pen.penup()
            pen.goto(x+30, y-30)
            pen.pendown()
            pen.circle(50)

draw_xo(0, 0, 'X')
draw_xo(1, 1, 'O')

screen.mainloop()
```

Run the program and observe the output. Study the following code to understand how the "X" is drawn:

```
pen.setheading(-45)
pen.forward(60)
pen.backward(120)
pen.forward(60)
pen.left(90)
```

Chapter 18 – X's and O's Take the Stage: Building Tic Tac Toe with Python

```
pen.forward(60)
pen.backward(120)
```

For drawing an "O", we'll simply draw a circle. The question now is: where do we start drawing from? We've determined this crucial position using the following two lines:

```
x = col * 200 - 300 + TILE_SIZE // 2
y = 300 - row * 200 - TILE_SIZE // 2
```

Understanding the Calculations

We know the screen size is 600 × 600 pixels. Therefore, each cell or tile measures 200 × 200 pixels. We've defined a `TILE_SIZE` variable with the value 200 at the beginning of the program.

Now, let's consider the case when row and col are both 0. What will the values of *x* and *y* be?

$$x = 0 \times 200 - 300 + \frac{200}{2}$$
$$= 0 - 300 + 100$$
$$= -200$$
$$y = 300 - 0 \times 200 - \frac{200}{2}$$
$$= 300 - 0 - 100$$
$$= 200$$

This means we'll move the turtle to the (−200, 200) position using `pen.goto(x, y)`. When drawing the circle, we'll shift slightly to the right and down to position the circle in the center of the cell.

Let's calculate the values of x and y when row = 1 and col = 1:

$$x = 1 \times 200 - 300 + \frac{200}{2}$$

$$= 200 - 300 + 100$$
$$= 0$$
$$y = 300 - 1 \times 200 - \frac{200}{2}$$
$$= 300 - 200 - 100$$
$$= 0$$

For this case, we'll move the turtle to the 0, 0 position on the screen, which is the exact center of the board. If you integrate the "X" and "O" drawing functionality into the board drawing program, you'll get an output like as shown on the right.

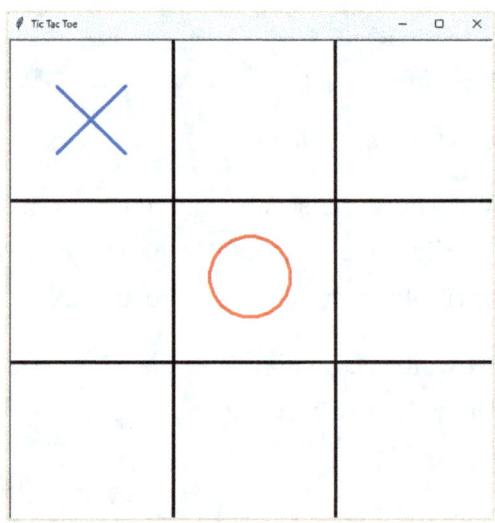

We have made significant progress in developing our Tic Tac Toe game. Now, let's tackle the next step: drawing an "X" or "O" in the cell where the mouse is clicked.

To manage the alternation between "X" and "O", we'll introduce a variable named `TURN`. We'll increment this variable's value by one after each turn. If the value is even, we'll draw an "X"; if it's odd, we'll draw an "O".

Now it's time to write the code for this:

```
import turtle

# set up the screen
```

Chapter 18 – X's and O's Take the Stage: Building Tic Tac Toe with Python

```python
screen = turtle.Screen()
screen.title("Tic Tac Toe")
screen.bgcolor("white")
screen.setup(width=600, height=600)

pen = turtle.Turtle()
pen.hideturtle()
pen.speed(8)
pen.width(4)

TURN = 0
TILE_SIZE = 200


def draw_line(x, y, length, angle):
    pen.penup()
    pen.goto(x, y)
    pen.setheading(angle)
    pen.pendown()
    pen.forward(length)
    pen.penup()


def draw_board():
    draw_line(-300, 100, 600, 0)
    draw_line(-300, -100, 600, 0)
    draw_line(-100, 300, 600, 270)
    draw_line(100, 300, 600, 270)


def draw_xo(row, col, player):
    x = col * 200 - 300 + TILE_SIZE // 2
    y = 300 - row * 200 - TILE_SIZE // 2
    pen.penup()
```

```python
        pen.goto(x, y)
        pen.pendown()
        if player == 'X':
            pen.color('blue')
            pen.setheading(-45)
            pen.forward(60)
            pen.backward(120)
            pen.forward(60)
            pen.left(90)
            pen.forward(60)
            pen.backward(120)
        elif player == 'O':
            pen.color('red')
            pen.penup()
            pen.goto(x+30, y-30)
            pen.pendown()
            pen.circle(50)


def on_click(x, y):
    global TURN
    col = int((x + 300) // 200)
    row = int((300 - y) // 200)
    player = 'X' if TURN % 2 == 0 else 'O'
    draw_xo(row, col, player)
    TURN += 1


draw_board()

turtle.onscreenclick(on_click)

screen.mainloop()
```

Chapter 18 – X's and O's Take the Stage: Building Tic Tac Toe with Python

The new `on_click()` function and `turtle.onscreenclick(on_click)` statement work together to capture mouse clicks on the screen. When a click occurs, the `on_click()` function is executed, receiving the x and y coordinates of the click location. From these coordinates, we can determine the corresponding row and column indices using the following formulas:

```
col = int((x + 300) // 200)
row = int((300 - y) // 200)
```

- The `col` variable represents the column index, ranging from 0 to 2.
- The `row` variable represents the row index, also ranging from 0 to 2.

This allows us to identify the specific cell where the click occurred and take appropriate actions based on the game rules.

To efficiently track the game's progress and check for winning conditions, we'll introduce a dictionary named `board`. This dictionary will store the state of each cell on the board, represented by a tuple of row and column indices and a corresponding value ("X", "O", or " ").

```
board = {(row, col): ' ' for row in range(3)
         for col in range(3)}
```

This code initializes the `board` dictionary with all cells set to an empty string (' '). As the game progresses, the dictionary will be updated to reflect the drawn symbols.

Now we need to find the winner. The `check_winner()` function determines if there's a winner or if the game is a draw. It systematically checks for winning patterns in rows, columns, and diagonals.

```python
def check_winner():
    # check rows, columns and diagonals for a winner
    for i in range(3):
        # check the i-th row
        if (board[(i, 0)] == board[(i, 1)] ==
                board[(i, 2)] != ' '):
            return board[(i, 0)]
        # check the i-th column
        if (board[(0, i)] == board[(1, i)] ==
                board[(2, i)] != ' '):
            return board[(0, i)]

    # check diagonal 1 (left to right)
    if (board[(0, 0)] == board[(1, 1)] ==
            board[(2, 2)] != ' '):
        return board[(0, 0)]
    # check diagonal 2 (right to left)
    if (board[(0, 2)] == board[(1, 1)] ==
            board[(2, 0)] != ' '):
        return board[(0, 2)]
    # check if all tiles are filled up
    # (no more space left)
    if all(board[(row, col)] != ' ' for row in range(3)
            for col in range(3)):
        return 'Tie'
    return None
```

This function iterates through rows, columns, and diagonals, checking for three consecutive symbols of the same type ("X" or "O"). If a winning pattern is found, it returns the winning symbol ("X", "O", or "Tie"). Otherwise, it returns `None` if no winner is found and the game continues.

By integrating the board dictionary and `check_winner()` function, we can effectively track the game state and determine the outcome of the Tic Tac Toe game. After each symbol is drawn, we can check the board using the `check_winner()` function to see if there's a winner or if the game is a draw.

If you've been following along, experimenting with the smaller code snippets and thinking along the way, you should have a good grasp of the overall structure and functionality of the complete Tic Tac Toe program. The code seamlessly integrates the various components we've discussed, including:

- *Setting up the screen and drawing the tic-tac-toe board:* The initial part of the code sets up the turtle graphics environment, draws the boundaries of the tic-tac-toe board, and positions the necessary lines to create the grid.
- *Handling mouse clicks and drawing symbols:* The `on_click()` function captures mouse clicks and determines the corresponding row and column indices. Based on these indices, the `draw_xo()` function draws the appropriate symbol ("X" or "O") in the corresponding cell.
- *Storing the board state in a dictionary:* The `board` dictionary efficiently stores the state of each cell on the board, represented by a tuple of row and column indices and a

corresponding value ("X", "O", or " "). This allows us to keep track of the game's progress.
- *Checking for winners:* The `check_winner()` function systematically checks for winning patterns in rows, columns, and diagonals. It returns the winning symbol ("X", "O", or "Tie") if a pattern is found, or `None` if no winner is determined.

By combining these components, the complete program provides a functional tic-tac-toe game that allows players to take turns marking their symbols and determines the outcome of the game.

```python
import turtle

# set up the screen
screen = turtle.Screen()
screen.title("Tic Tac Toe")
screen.bgcolor("white")
screen.setup(width=600, height=600)

TURN = 0
TILE_SIZE = 200

pen = turtle.Turtle()
pen.hideturtle()
pen.speed(8)


def draw_line(x, y, length, angle):
    pen.penup()
    pen.goto(x, y)
    pen.setheading(angle)
    pen.pendown()
```

```python
    pen.forward(length)
    pen.penup()


def draw_board():
    pen.width(4)
    draw_line(-300, 100, 600, 0)
    draw_line(-300, -100, 600, 0)
    draw_line(-100, 300, 600, 270)
    draw_line(100, 300, 600, 270)


# create a dictionary to store the board state
board = {(row, col): ' ' for row in range(3)
         for col in range(3)}


def draw_xo(row, col, player):
    x = col * 200 - 300 + TILE_SIZE // 2
    y = 300 - row * 200 - TILE_SIZE // 2
    pen.penup()
    pen.goto(x, y)
    pen.pendown()
    if player == 'X':
        pen.color('blue')
        pen.setheading(-45)
        pen.forward(60)
        pen.backward(120)
        pen.forward(60)
        pen.left(90)
        pen.forward(60)
        pen.backward(120)
    elif player == 'O':
        pen.color('red')
```

```python
        pen.penup()
        pen.goto(x+30, y-30)
        pen.pendown()
        pen.circle(50)


def check_winner():
    # check rows, columns and diagonals for a winner
    for i in range(3):
        # check the i-th row
        if (board[(i, 0)] == board[(i, 1)] ==
                board[(i, 2)] != ' '):
            return board[(i, 0)]
        # check the i-th column
        if (board[(0, i)] == board[(1, i)] ==
                board[(2, i)] != ' '):
            return board[(0, i)]

    # check diagonal 1 (left to right)
    if (board[(0, 0)] == board[(1, 1)] ==
            board[(2, 2)] != ' '):
        return board[(0, 0)]
    # check diagonal 2 (right to left)
    if (board[(0, 2)] == board[(1, 1)] ==
            board[(2, 0)] != ' '):
        return board[(0, 2)]
    # check if all tiles are filled up
    # (no more space left)
    if all(board[(row, col)] != ' ' for row in range(3)
            for col in range(3)):
        return 'Tie'
    return None
```

```python
def announce_winner(winner):
    turtle.clearscreen()
    pen.penup()
    pen.hideturtle()
    pen.goto(0, 0)
    if winner == 'Tie':
        pen.write("It's a tie!",
                  align="center",
                  font=("Arial", 32, "bold"))
    else:
        pen.write(f"{winner} wins!",
                  align="center",
                  font=("Arial", 32, "bold"))


def on_click(x, y):
    global TURN
    col = int((x + 300) // 200)
    row = int((300 - y) // 200)
    if ((row, col) in board and
            board[(row, col)] == ' '):
        player = 'X' if TURN % 2 == 0 else 'O'
        board[(row, col)] = player
        draw_xo(row, col, player)
        winner = check_winner()
        if winner:
            announce_winner(winner)
        else:
            TURN += 1

# initialize the game
draw_board()
```

```
turtle.onscreenclick(on_click)

screen.mainloop()
```

Congratulations on completing this programming journey! I hope you've enjoyed it as much as I have. Remember, programming is about problem-solving, persistence, and finding joy in the process. Keep pushing forward, embrace the power of community, and never stop learning. With dedication and passion, you can achieve remarkable things in the world of programming. Best of luck with your future endeavors and may your programming adventures continue to inspire and excite you!

The End

www.ingramcontent.com/pod-product-compliance
Lightning Source LLC
Chambersburg PA
CBHW071831210526
45479CB00001B/88